By the Gains of Industry

Birmingham Museums and Art Gallery 1885-1985

Stuart Davies

1985 Birmingham Museums and Art Gallery

The Publications Unit
City Museum and Art Gallery
Chamberlain Square
Birmingham B3 3DH

ISBN 0 7093 0131 6

Printed in England

Contents

Foreword

For a Local Authority Museum to publish a history
of itself must be an unusual event. Birmingham's
museums service is, however, one of the largest in
the country, and its history must reflect aspects of the
history of many other cities' museums. The importance
of early benefactors – the struggle to acquire significant
collections – the gradual replacement of private by
public funding for acquisitions – the growing importance of design, education and commercial activities –
all these things are part of a pattern which has been
repeated throughout the country. Ours is a typical
history, and as such will, we hope, be of interest far
beyond Birmingham.

But we hope and believe we are more than just
another typical museum service. We are proud of what
we have and what we do, and more than a little conscious of the debt we owe to those who built what we
are now privileged to curate. Private benefactors,
politicians, professional specialists and considerable
personalities have contributed to what now exists in
Birmingham. The centenary of the opening of the
first purpose-built museum in the City seems a good
moment for us to offer our thanks to all those involved.

This history has been written by Stuart Davies,
formerly Deputy Keeper of Local History. For his
completion of the project at a time when he has had
much else to occupy his mind, and to his usual
standard, we owe him our very special thanks.

Michael Diamond
Director

The Allen Everitt cabinet, presented to
him as a wedding gift.

Introduction

This book is intended to be neither a detailed catalogue of all that can be seen in Birmingham Museums (not possible) nor a definitive history of that institution (not necessary). It is a brief history illustrated mainly by some of the more attractive items in the collections chosen by the relevant curators but arranged according to their historical significance rather than by any academic or cultural criteria. Whether one judges it by collections, buildings or resources Birmingham can convincingly claim to have Britain's leading provincial museum. This year is the centenary of the opening of the present Central Museum and Art Gallery in Chamberlain Square, and this publication has been prepared to try to set the Museum as it is today in its historical context.

In this task I have received assistance from a large number of people. Most of my colleagues have given generously of their time and knowledge, but I particularly wish to thank Richard Lockett, Stephen Wildman, Brian Abell Seddon, Oliver Fairclough, George Learmonth, and John Warner-Davies, the City Archivist, who has been unfailingly helpful and supportive. Thanks are also due to Michael Diamond, Jack Henderson and Stephen Price, each of whom encouraged me to bring this study to fruition. I am pleased to acknowledge the assistance of a number of young people who have worked in the Department of Local History for varying lengths of time and have consequently been drawn into the preparatory work for this volume. Special thanks are therefore due to Karen Hull, Peter Jenkinson, Catherine Starkey, Michael Glasson, Rachel Wilkins and Celia Grant. Finally I wish to thank Trevor Jones for all his assistance in seeing this through to publication.

Stuart Davies

The Museum and Art Gallery, 1985.

This *View from the Dome of St Philip's*
(1821) gives an extraordinary idea of what
Birmingham was like at the time.

Early Days

No institutional history can be written without reference to the community which created, or was served by, that institution. Birmingham Museum's origin and early progress was determined by the aspirations and shortcomings of Birmingham's Victorian citizens. There was of course a national movement towards the foundation of municipal museums encouraged by Acts of Parliament passed in 1845 and 1850. The example of the National Museums, Central Government legislation, Literary Societies and some great local patrons of the Arts had all been responsible for establishing major museums elsewhere but their influence in Birmingham was negligible. It was the economic and political circumstances particular to the town in the second half of the nineteenth century which allowed what is now the most important provincial museum in Britain to develop.

Birmingham, a market town since the twelfth century and well known for its metal trades since the sixteenth century, underwent rapid industrialisation and urban growth during the late eighteenth and early nineteenth centuries. Its economy was based not on large factories, but on large numbers of small work-shops. These produced an astonishing variety of commodities designed both to appeal to the new mass markets at home and to the colonies abroad. Cheap metal utility goods of all kinds were made, but other industries concentrated on the fashion markets such as buttons, buckles, cut steel jewellery and papier mâché. These were often cheaply made to be within the pockets of a large proportion of the population, but some manufacturers concentrated on high quality products. Both, it was argued, needed to pay attention to 'good design', but few could afford to hire professional designers. The search for ways and means of raising the design quality of Birmingham products was the subject of much discussion in the mid-nineteenth century, partly stimulated by the 1849 Exhibition in Birmingham and, of course, by the Great Exhibition of 1851.

Politically, early-nineteenth-century Birmingham was backward. Only in 1832 did it obtain parlia-

Papier-mâché is well represented in the collections.

Birmingham Town Hall in about 1850.

mentary representation and it did not receive a Charter of Incorporation until 1838, which established a proper Town Council with elected members. Unfortunately, because of a legal dispute, it was not until 1851 that the Council was able to assume all its powers, and even then the controlling party declined, in the interests of economy, to exercise those powers. The more far-sighted citizens could only sit and wait for their opportunity. So it was that the 1840s and 1850s slipped away with very little corporate effort to improve the state of the town.

Birmingham was certainly ripe for improvement. Frenetic urban growth and industrialisation had meant that it had outstripped its facilities and services. Housing, sanitation and education were scandalously neglected. In the latter area the provision of schools was hopelessly inadequate and there had been no serious attempt to establish municipal libraries or museums for the broader education of the people.

There had been at least one small private 'museum', Bisset's in New Street, though it was more of a commercial enterprise than an educational establishment. Born in Perth in about 1762, Bisset had come to Birmingham when aged fifteen to become an artist's apprentice. By 1785 he was established as a 'miniature painter', a medallist and a writer of verse. A miniature of 1791 shows him in his shop surrounded by miniatures, buttons and other 'toys' which he sold. In 1808 he established his 'Museum and Picture Gallery' in New Street. His collection consisted principally of articles in natural history, including birds, crocodiles, rattlesnakes, 'the works of savage nations', and models in wax and rice-paste.

James Bisset's 'Museum' in New Street.

Bisset wrote the following lines when his museum first opened in Birmingham:

When first Museum struck the Public eye,
The wond'ring crowd, Unus'd such sights to 'spy,
About my windows flocking three-fold thick,
And squeezing close as ever they could stick,
The different articles their wonder raise,
And claim from most, at least some share of praise;
For be they Spars or polish'd Petrifaction,
Each in their turn affords them satisfaction.

In 1812 he moved to Leamington Spa, taking his museum with him. He died in 1832 and his collections are now lost.

The passing of a *Museums Act* in 1845 and the more extensive *Free Libraries and Museums Act* of 1850 aroused some citizens to begin agitation for the establishment of a Corporation Museum. The intellectual leaders of this movement were J. T. Bunce and W. C. Aitken. Bunce was apprenticed to the proprietor of the *Midland Counties Herald*, for which paper he eventually became a reporter. After fifteen years' service with the *Herald* he left in 1857 to briefly join the *Aris's Gazette*. In 1862 he became editor of the Liberal *Daily Post* and remained so until his death in 1899. His influence on many aspects of late Victorian Birmingham was enormous, but his main interest lay with the improvement of educational provision, implemented both nationally and locally through the Liberal Party. Aitken was a Superintendent successively at a brass and glass manufacturing firm

A medal advertising Bisset's 'Museum and Grand Picture Gallery' and a metal admission ticket to it.

Hardman plate and designs. Birmingham art manufacturers are well represented in the collections.

in Birmingham, but is mainly remembered for his numerous essays on the subject of Birmingham industries and on the importance of design in influencing the competitiveness of Birmingham products.

Bunce and Aitken argued at this time, and on many subsequent occasions, that good design was essential to the success of manufactured goods, especially in overseas markets. The artisans at work in Birmingham were being denied access to good examples of Industrial Art without which they could not fairly be expected to improve their designs. A School of Design had been established in Birmingham in 1843 but this was not enough. An Industrial Museum was needed in which examples of art objects could be displayed to give inspiration to the artisan. The appeal did not fall entirely on deaf ears, but a formal attempt to adopt the *Free Libraries and Museums Act* in Birmingham in 1852 failed, and the issue fell into abeyance.

However, a few months afterwards, the Birmingham and Midland Institute was founded. Among its objectives, the most important of which was to provide classes for artisans, was the opening of a 'Museum' and a 'Hall of Fine Arts'. In September 1853 the embryonic BMI took over the premises of the lately demised Philosophical Institution, including its 'museum'. The Philosophical Institution had developed from an association in 1800 of a number of scientifically-minded persons, many of whom had been friends and pupils of Joseph Priestley. By 1813 it had acquired buildings in Cannon Street, where a museum was established under the curatorship of William Ick. It closed its doors in 1849 and was officially wound up in 1852. The first thing that its new owners did was to dispose of much of the Institution's geological collections. The BMI started to build up a small collection of pictures and other art objects at the end of the 1850s and opened its own 'museum' in January 1860, and as such can claim to be the first public museum in Birmingham.

But meanwhile the political climate was changing and the prospects for a Corporation Museum and Art Gallery were much brighter. Throughout the 1850s the 'economist' party had controlled Birmingham Council. They resisted any civic improvement measures suggested by the more radical, enlightened members or municipal officials which would increase the rates. However the 'economists' suffered setback in the 1859 elections and the 'extravagant' party gained the advantage for two or three years. Thereafter the Tory 'economists' regained control until their final defeat in 1873 – but their policies were progressively more enlightened under intense pressure from the Liberal opposition. It is against this background that the initial push towards the establishment of a municipal museum and the subsequent slackening of pace must be seen.

On 21 February 1860 a Public Meeting held in the Town Hall and called by the Mayor at the request of the Town Council at last adopted the *Public Libraries and Museums Act* of 1850, despite opposition from the Birmingham Landlords' Association who called upon ratepayers to 'give this uncalled-for Measure their determined opposition'. A Committee (including

Edward Coleman's *Dead Game*, the first
painting presented to the Art Gallery.

Bunce and Aitken) was convened to set about im-
plementing the Act in Birmingham, beginning with
erecting a Library.

One problem which had to be faced was that the
Act allowed the raising of a rate only for building
and running the premises, but not for purchasing
collections. The Art Gallery (as it was always referred
to) would therefore have to rely on donations and
these were slow to come forward. In May 1863 the
Committee accepted a bust of David Cox by Peter
Hollins. During the following year two more important
gifts were offered. In a letter dated 7 October 1864,
Samuel Thornton (a JP and ex-Mayor) offered the
Corporation, as a gift for their proposed museum, a
7' 4"-high copper Buddha of *c*.400 A D, which had been
found at Sultanganj (India) in 1861. Six weeks later
Charles Cope, John Jaffray and Peter Hollins, on behalf

of a group of gentlemen subscribers, presented 'a fine Picture of Dead Game, by one of our most eminent local artists, the late Mr Edward Coleman'. They explained that the 'erection of a Gallery of Art, which the Council, with great wisdom and liberality, have sanctioned, seemed to invite such contributions as that we have the honour of presenting; and considering that the occupations of many of the people of Birmingham have a direct connection with the knowledge of the fine arts, it is to be hoped that the Gallery may soon be enriched with a collection of pictures that will not only be a representation of the skill of local artists, but may be the means of educating the tastes of those upon whom the reputation of Birmingham manufacturers chiefly depends'.

These acquisitions and a number of pictures on loan to the Corporation were first put on view to the public in 1865 but the 'Corporation Art Gallery' (a room 70 feet by 30 feet in the Central Library) was not officially opened until 1 August 1867. The collection consisted of fifty-six paintings, of which only about a dozen belonged to the Corporation.

In the following year a very fine collection of armour, jewellery and other pieces of applied art from the South Kensington Museum was temporarily exhibited in the Gallery. This created a great deal of interest: nearly 160,000 people visited the Gallery during the seven months when it was on show. The supporters of the Gallery were quick to grasp the importance of bringing in temporary exhibitions from elsewhere in order both to maintain interest in the new Gallery and to meet its objectives while funds were sought with which to create its own collections. In 1870 it was noted 'how the introduction of new objects, by gift and loan, increases and whets the desire to visit such places of amusement and instruction. To encourage the growth of taste, it is essential that those who are expected to produce the beautiful shall be surrounded by what is beautiful'.

Progress was undoubtedly slow in the 1860s. This was partly because 'economy' was still the watchword of the Council but also because the development of the Art Gallery was not among the highest priorities of the Liberals. It was, however, very much part of the overall concept of how Birmingham might be transformed.

Marble bust of David Cox, by Peter Hollins (1800-1886).

Those who helped establish the Gallery were also supporters of the wider 'civic gospel' propounded by nonconformist preachers and Liberal politicians. Dr Dale summed up the situation well, when, in later life, he recalled the beginning of the 'civic revolution' that came to fruition in Joseph Chamberlain's day: 'Towards the end of the 'sixties, a few Birmingham men made the discovery that perhaps a strong and able Town Council might do almost as much to improve the conditions of life in the town as Parliament itself . . . They spoke of sweeping away streets in which it was not possible to live a healthy and decent life; making the town cleaner, sweeter and brighter; of providing gardens and parks and music, of erecting baths and free libraries, an art gallery and a museum; . . . Sometimes an adventurous orator would excite his audience by dwelling on the glories of Florence, and of the other cities of Italy in the Middle Ages and suggest that Birmingham too might become the home of a noble literature and art.'

But the Art Gallery had to wait its turn. In the late 1860s the Liberals concentrated on forming the Birmingham Education League which spearheaded the movement which culminated in the passing of the great Education Act of 1870. When Joseph Chamberlain became Mayor and the Liberals won a landslide election victory in 1873 the municipalisation of gas and water, the slum clearance programme and the building of Corporation Street took precedence over the furthering of cultural activities.

Nevertheless, the 1870s did see some important developments. In March 1870 an Art Gallery Sub-Committee was formed, and it appointed Mr William Hall as Honorary Curator. In the same year, influenced by the success of the South Kensington Exhibition, an Appeal was launched to raise money to buy objects for an 'Industrial Art Museum', which was subsequently done during the following months.

Loans of pictures came and went, though gifts remained relatively few, which, to some at least, put in jeopardy the long-term prospects of the Art Gallery. William Sharp of Endwood Court, Handsworth, being 'desirous of having a better Gallery than the present one' made a gift of *Sunset in the Gulf of Salerno* by G. E. Herring, 'in the hope that others will follow me, in the pleasing exercise of the privilege, and make your task of obtaining a good collection the easier, by their voluntary offerings being promptly made'.

The reliance on individual gifts did, however, make the formation of a coherent collection very difficult, although some sort of collecting policy was imposed on the Gallery by the formation of the 'Public Picture Gallery Fund' for Birmingham in 1871. The Fund originated with a gift of £3000 from Thomas Clarkson Osler, a glass manufacturer, and was later supplemented by further donations from other citizens. Clarkson Osler had selected this cause for his personal benevolence because it seemed one unlikely to be provided for out of public funds. The hospitals, he considered, would be able to command sufficient voluntary support from the townsmen; responsibility for general education had been assumed by the State and was no longer dependent on private benevolence; but the maintenance of a Public Picture Gallery in Birmingham was unlikely to receive the aid it deserved, for there was little possibility that any income would be available from the rates for the acquisition of pictures – all that could be expected from that source would be needed for the purchase of books for the Free Libraries. This casts some light on how some of Birmingham's leading citizens viewed the promotion of an Art Gallery.

The Fund was administered by nine Trustees, the original ones nominated by Clarkson Osler. The practice of the Fund was for the Trustees to purchase a picture and then present it to the Corporation for the Art Gallery. The most important condition attached to the Fund was that the pictures purchased by it should be exhibited in a gallery open to the public without charge, including on Sundays. The practice of the Trustees was generally to purchase examples of work by living artists. The first picture, *A Condottière* by Frederick Leighton, was presented in 1873, and fourteen more followed before the end of the century.

Generally speaking the picture collections of the 1860s and 1870s have not been highly regarded by modern art historians. There was little 'professional' guidance in the selection of works for donation to the Gallery or acceptance by the Corporation. Many were portraits of local 'worthies', often paid for by subscription, or were pictures which had been publicly

Lord Leighton's *A Condottière*, the first painting presented to the Art Gallery by the Public Picture Gallery Fund.

Japanese tsuba (sword guards) are prominent among the oriental collections.

exhibited and were therefore assumed to be suitable for inclusion in the Gallery's permanent collections. Many, as was predicted by Joseph Chamberlain, a Trustee of the PPGF, were not to stand the test of time. In 1893 he expressed the view that it was unwise to buy pictures by living artists. 'Suppose', he said, 'that the Trustees had been in existence fifty years ago. They would have been justified by the current opinion of that time in buying at a large price, pictures by artists who were then much thought of but who have since been relegated to obscurity, and I am convinced that this will be the fate of a considerable number of men who are now represented in the Gallery.' Nevertheless, whilst this is undeniably true, it might also be argued that at least in the times before the arrival of professional curators the leading citizens of Birmingham would determine what they actually wanted to see in their Art Gallery.

Throughout the 1870s loans of industrial art for special exhibitions in Birmingham were negotiated with South Kensington and there was even an attempt to secure direct funding from central government. Permanent additions to the industrial art collections were rare with the exception of those items purchased in 1870-1. Then another benefactor stepped forward to give a boost to Birmingham's own collections. In April 1875 Joseph Chamberlain, Mayor and leader of the 'civic gospel' reformers, offered £1000 'to be expended . . . in the purchase of objects of Industrial Art, for permanent exhibition in the Art Gallery of the Town'. A small Purchase Sub-Committee was established to buy suitable objects, with the approval of Chamberlain. By the end of 1878 about three-quarters of this Purchase Fund had been spent, mostly on metalwork. Some of this had been manufactured in Birmingham but much was foreign. In March 1878, for example, the Sub-Committee 'purchased on account of the Chamberlain Fund for the sum of £180 a collection of Japanese ornamental silver and bronze collected in Japan by Mr R. B. Mitford, CB, formerly Her Majesty's Secretary of Legation in Japan.' Apart from these purchases there was one important gift. In 1876 the Guardians of the Birmingham Gun-Barrel Proof House resolved to transfer the Proof House Museum of Small Arms (a European collection) to the Corporation.

On 11 January 1879 the Reference Library was burnt down and among the losses was the 'Cervantes Library' given in 1873 by William Bragge, a notable benefactor and supporter of the Library. Within a few weeks of this disaster the Corporation decided to re-purchase from the Chamberlain Fund the objects already acquired and to commit the entire Fund of £1000 to the purchase of 'the collection of gems now in the possession of Mr Bragge'. Furthermore, the Art Gallery Committee purchased a collection of Russian Silver Chains and Chinese Sceptres from Mr Bragge for £200. So, not only was Chamberlain's £1000 to be spent on the Bragge collection of gems but the Corporation was in effect also providing nearly £1000 to purchase metalwork for the Art Gallery, a radical change in policy.

If the fire of January 1879 stimulated an increased liberality on the part of the Committee it certainly severely aggravated the Art Gallery's accommodation problems which had been mounting during the 1870s. As early as 1871 the Free Library Committee and the Midland Institute, as part of a rationalisation of their adjacent buildings, agreed that a first-floor Art Gallery and Industrial Museum would be included in plans to build a new theatre for the Institute. This plan was abandoned in 1875 when, in the wake of Chamberlain's gift, it was proposed to built a new Art Gallery on land in Edmund Street.

Meanwhile, however, major building works were being carried out in the Library (which still included the Art Gallery) and the Art Gallery collections would have to be temporarily housed in the Midland Institute rooms in Paradise Street. In January 1876 the Baths and Parks Department was requested to take charge of the Buddha at Aston Hall 'for safe custody during the re-building of the Art Gallery', but the remaining collections stayed in the Library. The rooms in Paradise Street were occupied at the end of the year by the 'Proof House Museum of Small Arms'.

This was the situation for over two years, but then in the spring of 1878 both the Art Gallery and the Paradise Street rooms were required by the builders. The Museum of Arms and the Corporation's own pictures were sent to Aston Hall, all loans were returned and small valuable items were deposited with the Birmingham Joint Stock Bank. Plans were

Birmingham was a major centre for the manufacture of guns and pistols.

proposed for the building of a new Art Gallery linked with the School of Art, but no progress was made for many months.

At the beginning of 1880 the Committee asked the Council to supply a piece of land as a site for the erection of a temporary Art Gallery. The decision to move the collections to Aston Hall had been necessary, 'but the result of it is that, owing to the distance of the collection from the great body of the population, the number of visitors has very largely fallen off, and the usefulness of the Art Gallery has consequently been seriously lessened . . . if the Art collections of the Corporation are to fulfil their purpose, they must be located in the centre of the town'. Aston Hall was also inadequate in that there was insufficient space to hang the pictures or exhibit the metalwork collection 'so that neither department can be properly seen, or much less studied by visitors'. They also made the point that unless exhibited properly the collections would not attract any further additions. All that was required for the moment was a temporary Art Gallery in the town centre ('this is scarcely the time to consider the provision of a permanent gallery'), and the Committee suggested that 'part of the unused space in the rear of the Council House might be allotted for this purpose'.

No progress was made for some months. Then, in July 1880, John Thackray Bunce received a letter from the Birmingham engineering firm, Tangye Brothers, written apparently by Richard Tangye on the firm's behalf. He referred to 'the great loss the town sustains in the absence of an adequate Art Collection' and then set out the case for its importance to Birmingham: 'We cannot but think if the Town and the Council were duly impressed with the vast importance of such a collection to the trades of the town, the present apathy on the subject would soon cease to exist. It is all very well for critics to exclaim against Birmingham manufacturers and artizans because of their inferiority to their foreign competitors in the matter of design, and manufacture, but what chance have they of improving in these respects? South Kensington is practically as far away as Paris or Munich, while our competitors on the Continent, in almost every manufacturing town, have access to collections containing the finest examples of art, furnishing an endless variety of style and design.'

He then went on to offer the Council, if they were 'to make provision for a permanent Art Gallery on a scale really commensurate with the necessities of Birmingham' the sum of £5000 for the purchase of objects of art and, if this were equalled by other donations, a further £5000 which he suggested should be invested, the interest only being available for purchases.

The response to this generous offer was immediate. The Council set about finding means of meeting Tangye's terms and offers of more help came in. Henry Buckley, for example, could not give a cash donation but offered instead 'the Cabinet of Coins and Medals, the property of the Soho Mint, and kept by them, I believe, for reference' which he had bought when the Mint's contents were sold. 'It contains many valuable pieces, and some that are all but unique, and in the event of the Council accepting Mr Tangye's noble offer I shall have great pleasure in transferring this collection to the town.' He concluded: 'I am sure, if a proper building is erected, you will find that so many of our Townsmen will contribute, that in a brief space we shall have an Art Gallery worthy of the town'.

In August the General Purposes Committee reported on their investigation into how a permanent Art Gallery and Museum might be provided for the town. They were agreed that the best site was the land at the rear of the Council House, fronting to Edmund Street, Congreve Street and Eden Place. Since 1865 this had been earmarked for new Assize Courts but an expansion of the Council's offices was now considered more important. Unfortunately, the Free Libraries Committee was not legally empowered to build an Art Gallery on the site because it was constituted under the *Public Libraries and Museums Act* of 1850 which limited its expenses to the penny rate, a sum inadequate to erect a substantial building.

However, under Section 18 of the Act, the Council was allowed, 'in addition to, and independently of, the penny rate, with the approval of Her Majesty's Treasury, to appropriate for the purposes of that Art any lands vested in the Corporation, and the Council may, upon any land so appropriated, erect buildings for Public Libraries or Museums, or both, or for Schools for Science or Art.' Now, one of the Council's objec-

An invitation card to the laying of the Art Gallery's 'Inscription Stone' in 1881.

tives was to bring together all its departments on one site. At that time most of them were in the Council House, but the Gas and Water Departments were separate. The opportunity to deal with two problems at once was now grasped. 'Your Committee are strongly of opinion that it is very desirable in the interests of the public service, that offices for the Gas Department should be provided in connection with the Council House, and the Gas Committee having regard to the great importance of providing an Art Gallery and Museum for the town without delay, have cordially approved of the suggestion that they should erect offices for their department, and, at the expense of their department, provide on the first or upper floor an Art Gallery and Museum . . .' Thus was Birmingham to get its new Art Gallery, built by the Gas Committee as a means of evading the terms of the *Public Libraries and Museums Act*.

Building work began immediately, plans were drawn up and all knew that 'the town will, at no distant period, be in possession of a building adequate to its requirements, and second only to the galleries in which the national collections are exhibited'. By April 1881 it was decided that the time had come to start 'the work of selecting objects of Art for the Art Gallery'. Thanks in no small degree to the efforts of the Mayor (Mr Richard Chamberlain) about £7000 had been raised in addition to the Tangyes' £10,000. An Art Gallery Purchase Committee was formed and the first written collecting policy was produced, incorporating the guidelines upon which the Art Gallery and Museum would develop.

It was hoped that the Museum would acquire 'a thoroughly representative character as regards the historic development of Art, both pictorial and ornamental, keeping in view, as their main objects, the cultivation of public taste, and the benefit of designers and others engaged in the trades of the town'. As far as Fine Art was concerned the Committee hoped to supplement the collections through occasional purchases, gifts and the PPGF, while depending heavily on loans to maintain interesting exhibitions. They thought it 'especially desirable that the works of Birmingham artists who have risen to eminence should be represented in the galleries, and particularly so as regards Birmingham engravers . . .'

The funds at the disposal of the Committee were, however, to be 'mainly applied to the provision of objects of Industrial Art'. The principle to be applied in the selection of material was that 'all attainable objects of historic interest, of artistic quality, and of practical suggestiveness, should be included in the Corporation galleries; all indeed, that can extend the knowledge, refine the taste, instruct the judgement, and strengthen the faculty of those who are engaged in Birmingham industries should be provided for the free and constant study and use of all'. The main areas of collections were identified as precious metals, jewellery, brass work, iron work, glassware and arms of all kinds.

Jewellery by Hardman, purchased from the Bingley Hall Exhibition in 1886.

In carrying out this policy the Purchase Committee sought the advice and help of 'experts' in London. J. C. Robinson, Her Majesty's Surveyor of Pictures, made a trip to Italy in the summer if 1883 where he collected works for Birmingham including medieval Venetian objects 'embracing a great variety of subjects and styles of treatment, all of which are well adapted for the instruction of designers and artizans in the various trades conducted in Birmingham'. Robinson anticipated that some of his purchases might be questioned on grounds of relevance to Birmingham's metalwork but he had his answers ready. 'If it should be asked what use Italian sculptures, marble saints and madonnas, terracotta busts, carved pilasters and friezes, chimney pieces and cassoni, are likely to be to Birmingham and its working thousands my answer is that I entirely refuse to admit that art culture in the provinces should be a different thing, or pitched at a lower level than in London' and that Italian works of art are full of 'infinite instruction to art workmen, modellers, carvers, die sinkers, chasers, art metal workers, and craftsmen in every branch.' In the same year Japanese enamels were purchased from Frederick Elkington, the silver manufacturer, and another gem collection was acquired. Finally, 1883 also saw the beginnings of what was to become Birmingham's most famous collection: 'Your Committee have to express their obligations to Messrs Agnew and Son, of Old Bond Street, London, for the valuable assistance rendered by them in acquiring, at the recent sale of works by Dante Gabriel Rossetti, two fine drawings

(overleaf) Whitworth Wallis in his office.

entitled *Lady of Pity* and *The Boat of Love'*.

By December 1884 the building was 'in a very forward state' and the Committee turned its attention to appointing a Keeper for the Art Gallery. They decided that they needed someone from the National Museum at South Kensington, the Director of which recommended Mr Whitworth Wallis. He was aged thirty, the second son of Mr George Wallis, Keeper of the Art Collections at South Kensington (and formerly well known in Birmingham for his valuable services as the first Master of the Birmingham School of Art). Whitworth had spent some time in Germany and France before coming to South Kensington in 1879.

The building, which had been designed by Mr H. Yeoville Thomason (who had also been the architect of the adjoining Council House opened in 1879), was soon completed and handed over to Whitworth Wallis, whose task was to display the collections. The visitor would enter at ground floor level and then ascend a fine staircase into a vestibule. This led into the 'Round Room' in the corners of which were located the staff offices. Beyond this was the 'Italian Gallery' (today's Coin Gallery) which led to the 'Industrial Hall' with its balconies on the longer sides. Between this and the long 'Picture Gallery' was another small gallery.

The Art Gallery was finally opened on 28 November 1885 by the Prince of Wales (later King Edward VII). Forty years had passed since J. T. Bunce had first appealed for a Corporation Art Gallery in Birmingham. He and many others had always argued that such an institution would be of principal benefit to the artisans of the town, but in the end it was the generosity of manufacturers that secured it for the town. Thus it is that a memorial stone in the entrance hall bears these appropriate words: 'By the gains of Industry we promote Art'.

Building up Collections

The building of an Art Gallery and the appointment of a professional curator were of fundamental importance to the growth of the city's collections. The Art Gallery's new status naturally attracted a substantial increase in donations. Not all of these were solicited but Wallis certainly attempted to lead potential benefactors in particular directions. He was to be Keeper for over forty years, so his personal influence on collection development can hardly be overestimated. Similarly the Art Gallery Purchase Committee, set up to utilise the funds donated by the Tangyes (and others) for the purchase of objects, was also influential, not least of all because these purchases became the foundation collections upon which much of what came afterwards automatically built.

A major characteristic of the objects purchased is its bewildering variety. There is a distinct apparent lack of organisation or method in what was being acquired. This is simply because the idea was not to put together collections representing certain subjects, themes or periods from the past, but rather to collect skilfully designed or artistically fine objects which would be of assistance to the Birmingham artisan.

They certainly went to considerable lengths in pursuing this broad policy. In 1886 Whitworth Wallis travelled to Egypt and Italy where he purchased 'Persian and Damascus metal work and tiles, and numerous specimens of 16th and 17th century iron work.' Wallis made two further trips to Italy in 1887 and 1889, mainly purchasing metal work (which of course was always considered important in relation to Birmingham industries). Much of the material purchased was modern. It was considered important because industrialisation had not yet obscured traditional forms of craftsmanship. The outlay on these trips was substantial and the objects purchased on the 1889 expedition cost over £900. Wallis also made some small purchases from Germany in 1891 when, presumably, he was on a private visit.

The Committee was conscious of the fact that the funds at its disposal were limited. In 1887, for example, Councillor Beale reported that the whole of the gallery space available was occupied with 'renowned and

valuable collections' and there was no shortage of people prepared to loan collections. The Committee had therefore used the funds 'to secure such works and Art Collections as they considered likely to prove valuable for educational purposes, and which they were able to obtain at reasonable cost'. Beale spoke of 'the formation of a thoroughly representative and educational Museum and Art Gallery . . .' and emphasised that '. . . the prices have . . . been generously and materially reduced'·on some purchases.

When first established the Committee had taken the initiative of commissioning two works. The one, *The Star of Bethlehem* by Sir Edward Burne-Jones, was completed in 1891 at a cost of £2000. His widow was later to recall that 'the commission received from his native place to paint a picture for it was a source of lasting pleasure and satisfaction'.

By 1914 Birmingham had built up certain collections by which it was 'especially distinguished and has acquired a national importance . . . The work of David Cox and Sir Edward Burne-Jones is now more largely represented in the public gallery of their native town than in any other place; and the gallery affords opportunities, not to be found elsewhere, for studying the art of the Pre-Raphaelite Brotherhood and of other English artists classified as of the same school'. In 1912, eighty-three of the Pre-Raphaelite pictures and drawings were borrowed by the Tate Gallery as a special exhibition, and attracted the attention of a very large number of visitors.

What had been the essential causes of this actually rather unlikely distinction attaching itself to Birmingham? The collection of works by local artists can simply be explained by local pride. Birmingham's association with a famous collection of Pre-Raphaelite paintings is more surprising since, although some were exhibited in the town in the mid-nineteenth century, none were acquired by Birmingham collectors until much later. Indeed it was not until the 1880s that some great civic families responded to the Pre-Raphaelite paintings and were encouraged by Whitworth Wallis to present such works of art to the Gallery.

Once established, a distinctive collection will tend to attract further examples because of the desire to build up a prestigious group of works in that particular field.

(opposite) David Cox, the Birmingham artist.

Holman Hunt's *The Finding of the Saviour in the Temple* was amongst the 'first wave' of Pre-Raphaelite paintings presented to Birmingham.

But to get started it needs some particular circumstance or encouragement. In the case of the Birmingham collection the 1891 exhibition may have been extremely influential, for in that year no fewer than six Pre-Raphaelite paintings were purchased for the collection and another was added by William Kenrick, Chairman of the Art Gallery Committee.

The Purchase Committee certainly contributed to the building up of the Pre-Raphaelite Collection. In 1887 they purchased *Two Gentlemen of Verona* by W. Holman Hunt (painted in 1851), 'a most valuable addition to the Art Treasures of the town'. Four years later, 1891, saw the acquisition of *The Last of England* by Ford Madox Brown, *Beata Beatrix* by Rossetti, *A Widow's Mite* by Millais, two works by Arthur Hughes and one by J. F. Lewis. Birmingham Art Gallery staged an *English Pre-Raphaelite Exhibition* in 1891. The Millais and the two by Hughes were exhibited in it. The Committee purchased thirteen oil paintings between 1886 and 1899, six of which were by major Pre-Raphaelite painters. Just over £7000 was spent on these, while nearly £10,000 was spent on Industrial Art. The Committee did buy a number of watercolours

The staff of the Art Gallery in about 1900.

between 1890 and 1892, including *The Falls of Schaff-hausen* by J. M. W. Turner in 1891. At the commencement of 1893 Alderman Kenrick presented two watercolours, noting that the Purchase Committee had decided to establish a collection of watercolours, 'this delightful and peculiarly British Art . . .' He believed that there were 'many valuable and interesting private collections' in Birmingham which, through gifts and bequests, could be drawn upon to build up a collection in the Art Gallery. The Committee evidently agreed, for from that moment on it virtually ceased to purchase watercolours.

Nevertheless, the purchases made of paintings by the Pre-Raphaelites and also of watercolours did form the beginning of major collections which were added to by gift and (much later) by more purchases. Early in 1892 William Kenrick presented *The Blind Girl* by Millais, as a memorial of the Pre-Raphaelite exhibition of the year before. Then in 1896 J. T. Middlemore offered Holman Hunt's *Finding the Saviour in the Temple*, writing that 'I am glad I am able to offer a Pre-Raphaelite work, as our City is becoming – possibly has already become – the best centre in the world in

which to study this distinctively English School of Art'. The Council accepted his offer, remarking about the work, '... which as illustrating one of the highest developments of English Art, confers unique distinction upon the Birmingham Art Gallery'.

In some ways Middlemore's claim might be considered rather extravagant, for the Pre-Raphaelite collection was still quite modest, though Birmingham could claim to be a centre for Pre-Raphaelite artists, but much was yet to come. Middlemore was to add two more works in 1903 and 1912, the Public Picture Gallery Fund offered three pictures by Ford Madox Brown in 1915-16 and two works were bequeathed by J. R. Holliday in 1927. Other gifts during the first quarter of the twentieth century contributed substantially towards making the Pre-Raphaelite paintings collection what it is today.

There were a number of important additions in 1898. Alderman Kenrick and Mr J. R. Holliday jointly presented three cartoons for stained-glass by Sir Edward Burne-Jones. At the same time the same artist's *Elijah* was given by Sir John Holder, Mr J. T. Middlemore, and Mr John Feeney. At the sale in 1898 of the works of Burne-Jones several examples were acquired by the Art Gallery Purchase Committee and Mr Charles Fairfax Murray presented six large cartoons for stained-glass windows by Burne-Jones and two by William Morris. It could be claimed indeed, that the real strengths of Birmingham's Pre-Raphaelite Collections were the drawings and cartoons. Major contributions were made by two groups of subscribers in 1903 and 1906. In May 1903 no fewer than 260 drawings, studies and sketches by Rossetti and 226 by Sir Edward Burne-Jones were presented by a group of five benefactors: J. R. Holliday, William Kenrick, C. A. Smith-Ryland, John Feeney and Cregoe Colmore. In 1906 a further 300 drawings by Millais, Madox Brown and Sandys were given by a group of eight (different) benefactors.

The growth of the Pre-Raphaelite collections was not entirely a smooth one. In 1898 John T. Middlemore M P wrote to J. T. Bunce offering to present to the City a number of important works by Burne-Jones, *The Triumph of the Innocents* by Holman Hunt and *Aspiration* by G. F. Watts, 'if our city will build what I

D. G. Rossetti's *The First Anniversary of the Death of Beatrice* (1849) was presented by a group of subscribers in 1904.

(opposite) John Millais' *Blind Girl* was the gift in 1892 of William Kenrick, the influential Chairman of the Art Gallery Committee.

consider a suitable gallery for the proper display of the works of art which it possesses, and hopes to possess . . .' He concluded his letter with an ominous postscript: 'May I add that the above offer will be withdrawn if there is what I consider undue delay in the Council's sanction of a new gallery or in its erection?'

The Committee reported that 'this is the most important collection of works of art which has been presented to any municipality since Sir Henry Tate gave the principal contents of the National Gallery of British Art to the nation', and set about investigating the provision of an extension to the Art Gallery. However, nothing materialised and in 1901 Middlemore withdrew his offer. Within a few months he had withdrawn those works on loan to the Art Gallery and sent them to Manchester, to Sheffield or to his residence at Belbroughton. Among those works originally offered was the *Pygmalion and Image* series of four paintings. In 1903 he wrote to the Lord Mayor, having heard that 'several of our fellow-citizens are proposing to give Birmingham a unique and invaluable collection of drawings by Rossetti and Burne-Jones'. He now offered the Pygmalion series, (which had been loaned to Nottingham Art Gallery), without conditions. One cannot help but suspect that he did not wish to be seen to be ungenerous in the circumstances.

Although this period is best known for the establishment of the Pre-Raphaelite collections it is important to remember that other subject areas were also endowed through gifts. The works of nineteenth-century British artists continue to be well represented, with a special emphasis on those who exhibited at the Royal Academy during the last quarter of the century. Similarly, the pictures presented by the Trustees of the Public Picture Gallery Fund are almost exclusively post-1850.

There was also an emphasis on the works of Birmingham artists. Burne-Jones was, as has been seen, well represented and additions to the Cox collection bequeathed by Nettlefold in 1882 were made. In 1907, for example, J. R. Holliday, on behalf of eleven subscribers, presented a collection of 105 drawings by Cox. 'On his death, early in the year 1913, it was announced that he had bequeathed eighty-four pictures, including thirty-one works of David Cox, to the Gallery, the legacy to take effect on the death of Mrs Phillips.'

In 1903 Phillips presented three oils by C. T. Burt, the last surviving pupil of David Cox. The mid-nineteenth-century works of F. H. Henshaw, who was born and worked mainly in Birmingham, are also well represented. Forty-two drawings of 'Old Birmingham' by Samuel Lines, S. R. Lines, F. T. Lines and H. H. Lines, were presented in 1893 by Mr F. T. Lines.

The practice of presenting portraits of Birmingham worthies paid for by public subscription continued during this period. In this way the Art Gallery acquired portraits of Alderman C. G. Beale and Alderman William Kenrick. Mention must also be made of the watercolour drawings by T. M. Rooke, presented by the subscribers to the Society for the Preservation of Pictorial Records and Works of Art.

The motives behind the gifts to the Art Gallery must have been numerous, but many were intended to serve the purposes of commemorating the names of well-known citizens. For example, two paintings by Albert Moore (1877 and 1878) from the Joseph Chamberlain collection were presented in his memory (in 1914) by Austen and Neville Chamberlain.

By all these means Birmingham Art Gallery built up a substantial collection of British paintings of the second half of the nineteenth century. This was achieved partly because the 'taste' of Birmingham collectors was for works of this period and partly because it was actively encouraged by Whitworth Wallis himself.

The Industrial Art collections were mostly acquired by the Art Gallery Purchase Committee, who between 1885 and 1899 spent nearly £10,000 on objects of industrial and decorative art. There were, however, a number of important gifts in 1885 itself. Richard and George Tangye presented a collection of 184 pieces of Wedgwood pottery; Messrs Elkington donated several bronzes 'of their own manufacture'; and Mr John Feeney presented the first instalment of his collection of objects illustrating the art of many nations, but 'especially rich in Oriental and Asiatic work'. Other gifts were to include a fine collection of Italian carved stone capitals presented by Sir Charles Robinson and

Stained glass by Francis Eginton, one of the most well known of Birmingham manufacturers who specialised in this product.

(overleaf) The Industrial Gallery at the end of the nineteenth century.

a collection of Birmingham jewellery and metalwork from the 1887 Bingley Hall Exhibition Committee.

As for the purchased items, mention has already been made of Whitworth Wallis's trips abroad. 'In 1886-7 collections of Persian and Damascus ware were purchased by him in Egypt, and many objects from private sources, and from the Indian and Colonial Exhibition. In 1889 Mr Wallis made a special journey, extending over some months, to Southern Italy, Sicily, Tuscany, Umbria, the Marches, and Venezia, acquiring valuable objects in gold, silver, bronze, and other metals, jewellery, textiles and embroideries, glass, carvings in marble, stone, and wood, and decorative ironwork.'

Items were purchased from individuals, such as the collection of Venetian glass from Sir Charles Robinson, but the Committee also bought items at major sales of collections such as Magniac, Spitzer and Bardini. The range of items was broadly within European metal-work and glass. French and German work was well represented but it was the Italian items which pre-dominated. There were plenty of exceptions to this broad picture, such as Indian textiles and 'Ancient Peruvian Pottery'.

The activities of the Art Gallery Purchase Committee and the interests of most Birmingham benefactors were of course directed towards the establishing of a permanent collection. However even in the old Art Gallery temporary exhibitions had an important role, allowing items from South Kensington to be seen in Birmingham. From 1885 to 1903 there was an almost uninterrupted series of major annual loan exhibitions. The subjects covered included artists with Birmingham connections, such as Edward Burne-Jones (1885), Walter Langley (1886), F. H. Henshaw (1886), and David Cox (1890); Old Masters (1888 and 1889); British Animal and Marine Painters (1892 and 1894); the English Pre-Raphaelites (1891); W. J. Muller (1896); J. M. W. Turner (1899); English Eighteenth-century Artists (1900 and 1903). There was also a 'Special Exhibition of Decorative Art' in 1896.

This was an outstandingly successful series of exhibitions. All of them were seen by 100,000 visitors in the first three months after they were opened and four ('Pictures by English artists', 'Family Portraits and

The Round Room at the beginning of this century.

Works by Old Masters', 'English Pre-Raphaelite School' and 'English Animal Painters') exceeded 200,000. Most spectacular of all was the first in 1885, ('Paintings by G. F. Watts and Sir Edward Jones') which topped 400,000. Clearly the latter was influenced by the fact that the Art Gallery had just opened, but it can be seen that for nearly twenty years these exhibitions were visited by large numbers of people. In 1891, for example, well over one-third of the year's visitors came during the first three months of the Pre-Raphaelite exhibition.

The exhibition of 'Decorative Art' included modern tapestries, designs for stained glass and examples of bookbinding and typography. It displayed the work, among others, of Burne-Jones, Ford Madox Brown, Rossetti and William Morris. It 'attracted a great amount of attention' and 1400 copies of the penny catalogue were sold. The national importance of some of the exhibitions cannot be denied. The W. J. Muller exhibition, for example, consisting of two hundred of

The Elgin Vase, presented by Sir Benjamin Stone, glass manufacturer, photographer and benefactor of the Museum.

(opposite) Francis Towne's *Near Naples* (1781) presented by the Public Picture Gallery Fund in 1921.

his works, '. . . proved to be attractive in the highest degree, visitors travelling from all parts of England to see it, as it formed the most complete collection ever held of this artist's work'.

The first year in which no special exhibition was held at the Art Gallery was 1893. The reason for this was that it was considered necessary to completely clean and re-paint the Art Gallery: 'With the exception of the partial cleaning of the Long Room, nothing has been done in this matter since the opening of the Gallery in November, 1885, and the rooms are consequently in such a dirty condition as to be unsightly, to greatly impede the work of the attendants in keeping the collections free from dust, and in causing a distinct loss of light'.

The special exhibitions resumed in the following year, but ceased again after 1903 because of inadequate space in the galleries. In 1900 the Committee drew '. . . the serious attention of the Council to the present overcrowded state of the building and to the fact that valuable pictures and art objects cannot be properly displayed. They also find it impossible to arrange for Loan Exhibitions to the same extent and importance as those held in past years, and this has greatly reduced the annual number of visitors. If the Birmingham Art Gallery is to maintain its present position amongst provincial galleries, efforts must be made to provide increased accommodation.' They repeated their plea in 1901. Not only could the collections not be properly displayed, but 'The Officials of the Victoria and Albert Museum have also drawn the attention of your Committee to the great inconveniences and risk of packing and unpacking valuable and fragile objects in the present inadequate space'. They concluded that increased accommodation was essential if Birmingham Art Gallery was to maintain its position among provincial galleries.

There was little that could be done substantially to improve the existing building. In 1893-4 the four spiral staircases in each corner of the Industrial Gallery were removed. They were replaced by a large T-shaped staircase and two linking balconies (or 'bridges') at either end of the Gallery. 'These alterations have greatly facilitated the exhibition of objects and the removal of the small staircases has provided a slight additional

'The Bridge' between the old and new galleries in 1912.

amount of floor space. The new staircase and bridges are much appreciated by the public, large numbers of visitors ascending to the galleries, whereas formerly the objects there were seldom inspected.' As already noted, the whole Art Gallery was cleaned and re-painted at the same time. All objects in the permanent collections were cleaned and the collections re-arranged, decorative ironwork being removed from the Long Gallery into the Italian Gallery.

The Art Gallery Committee continued to investigate the use of electric lighting, but in 1902 concluded that the Long Gallery could be 'more effectively' lit by gas rather than electricity. But in order to meet the terms of the Nettlefold Bequest of Cox paintings they decided to have electric lighting installed in the Round Room.

The solution to the problem of space could only be a major extension to the existing building, and that only in conjunction with the needs of other Corporation departments. Within twenty years of being completed the Council House was already overcrowded and an extension was needed. In 1899 the Corporation purchased a site adjacent to the Council House and Art Gallery from the Colmore Trustees. Work began on clearing the site in 1904 and space within the proposed new building, known as the Council House Extension, was allocated in 1905. The first phase of the extension was to build three sides of a quadrilateral. The east or Margaret Street side was allotted to the Education Department, the south or Edmund Street side to the Gas Department, and the western side facing Congreve Street was given to the new offices of the Health, the Housing, and the Tramways Committees. The Gas Department was to vacate entirely its offices on the other side of Edmund Street, and those offices were to be transferred to the Water Department. It would occupy the basement and ground floor of the Edmund Street wing of the extension, leaving the upper floor for the proposed enlargement of the Art Gallery. The top floor on the Congreve Street front was not wanted by the departments, and, 'being accessible from the new Art Gallery might be appropriated to a Museum of Natural History'. The Great Charles Street side of the extension was to be built later.

Then, in 1905, John Feeney, the proprietor of the *Birmingham Daily Post* and a major civic benefactor,

died. In his will he bequeathed £50,000 for the erection of an Art Gallery. During his lifetime he had presented a large number of objects to the gallery and had served as a Trustee of the PPGF. After due consideration it was decided that the Corporation should go ahead with the erection of the Council House Extension as planned, appropriating the Feeney bequest to provide a new suite of galleries, to be known as the 'Feeney Art Galleries' on the upper floors.

In 1910 the Feeney Charitable Trust provided funds for the purchase of a collection of casts, models, reproductions, and photographs to illustrate classical art. A condition of the grant was that suitable accommodation for the 'Museum of Casts' must be found by the Corporation. It was therefore allocated space in the Great Charles Street side of the Council House Extension, forming part of the overall memorial to John Feeney.

During the Great War many of the most valuable pictures and objects were stored in places of safety, but

William Blake's *The Circle of the Lustful* (1824-7) presented by the Public Picture Gallery Fund in 1919.

Japanese prints in the collection include *The Awabi Fishers* by Utamaro, bequeathed to Birmingham in 1926.

(above, right) John Martin's *Manfred on the Jungfrau* (1837) presented by A. E. Anderson in 1922.

the galleries nevertheless remained open to the public until July 1918 when they were requisitioned for the 'purposes of National Service'. The existing galleries and the new Feeney galleries were not fully available until the end of 1919. In the following year Sir Whitworth Wallis reached retirement age but he was invited to retain his Keepership out of recognition of the achievements of the previous thirty-five years. The same thing happened again in 1923 and so when his death occurred on 16 January 1927 he was still Keeper of the Art Gallery.

Wallis's influence on the Art Gallery was prodigious. Not only was he the first professional Curator, but his influence on the development of the art collections was to have lasting consequences for Birmingham Museum and Art Gallery. It was perhaps he who could claim most of the responsibility for the establishing of Birmingham as a centre for Pre-Raphaelite art, possibly at the expense of Industrial Art which those who had founded the Art Gallery considered much the more important. Art was certainly his principal interest and it could be argued that a 'Natural History Museum' came into existence in 1913 despite Sir Whitworth rather than because of him. Nevertheless, his years as Keeper in Birmingham certainly gave the Museum and Art Gallery a position of pre-eminence among provincial museums and art galleries which his successors could build upon.

Birmingham and the Natural World

Practical application of knowledge of the 'Natural World' has a long history in Birmingham, beginning with William Withering's digitalis research in the late eighteenth century. Indeed the medical profession was responsible for preserving some early private collections in the town. Mr Weaver, a bootmaker in New Street, became a taxidermist in Bromsgrove Street in 1841 and then set up his Natural History Collection in Temple Street. This collection was purchased for £1500 by Queen's College who held specimens at their premises in Paradise Street, which were apparently open to inspection by the public. Mr Sands Cox left his own collection of natural history specimens to Queen's when he died. Finally, Mason College, the forerunner of the University, had its own Geological Museum.

Natural history societies also had an important influence on the development of a museum. In 1858 the Birmingham Natural History Association was founded, its purpose being 'the mutual instruction of its members, the furtherance of a knowledge of Natural History, and the acquirement of a museum and library'. Many of the early members were important and res-pected people in the town. In 1864 it changed its name to the Birmingham Natural History and Microscopi-cal Society and purchased several cases of insects and some books. Some of its early members are said to have actively supported the idea of establishing a natural history museum in Birmingham, the most prominent being W. G. Blatch (died 1891), a part of whose 'Collection of Midland Coleoptera' may have eventually found its way into the City Museum. There were evidently numerous calls for the founding of a mu-seum during the 1880s and 1890s. In 1894 the Society amalgamated with the Birmingham Philosophical Society to form the Birmingham Natural History and Philosophical Society. But in practical terms nothing had been achieved towards the foundation of a Natural History Museum in Birmingham by the end of the century. At the beginning of 1898 five natural history societies and the Council of Mason University College all petitioned the Council to set up a Natural History Museum. In 1899 it was pointed out that 'There is in Birmingham a very large and important Natural

History Society, whose members have pursued their favourite study for a great many years with beneficial results, but their work would have been more useful and effective from an educational point of view if there had been in the City a natural history museum accessible to the people on the same lines as the Industrial Museum and Art Gallery. The city in this respect is very much behind other places'.

Progress would probably have continued to be painfully slow had it not been for a little controversy surrounding the natural history collections at Aston Hall. In 1869 the Queen's College collections had been transferred to the Corporation and housed at damp Aston Hall, 'as undesirable a place for a museum as can be well imagined'. Thirty years later it was alleged that the collections had so deteriorated that most of them had been consigned to a 'diabolical bonfire'. This was convincingly refuted by Whitworth Wallis who claimed that only a few specimens had been destroyed. Others had been re-arranged in a smaller space or had been only removed from public view. He and E. H. Spicer the taxidermist, were between them able to account for the fate of some of the most popular exhibits. Two giraffes had indeed been destroyed. 'Their bodies consisted of shavings, horsehair and bed-ticking, in which were a quantity of mice, and the backbone of the male animal was the top or front of a Birmingham cast-iron fender.' The 'great mischief was done in removing them. The necks and legs were sawn off to enable them to be got out of the college, and they were not very successfully put together again.' As to the hippopotamus, rhinoceros and the crocodiles, they had been removed to the upper rooms and out of public view 'because they were being mutilated by youthful visitors' and they were in any case considered out of keeping with the architecture of the entrance hall. The *Nestor productus* (Phillip Island Parrot), a rare skin of an extinct bird, was also safe.

Although the scare was largely groundless, it did fuel the agitation for a proper Natural History Museum in the city. In 1904 a petition in favour of the idea, supported by the heads of all the public educational institutions in the city, was presented to the Council. The time seemed right, for the city had just acquired the Council House Extension site. The petition pointed out

(opposite) The Great Auk, a rare specimen from the Natural History collections.

that several important collections had already been lost to the city for want of a suitable building in which to deposit them, and also the educational and humanising value of a natural history museum. As the *Birmingham Daily Mail* was later to observe, Birmingham had never lacked for knowledgeable men or societies devoted to the natural sciences, but it was another thing to persuade the City Council 'to realise that the study of insects, birds and fossils is something more than a harmless form of madness' and to spend money on a museum. Although the petition was well received, however, nothing was actually done. The real 'break-through' did not come for another five years. In 1909 Mr H. Willoughby Ellis, an amateur geologist, delivered the Presidential Address to the Birmingham Natural History and Philosophical Society, largely on the subject of 'the urgent necessity for a Municipal Natural History Museum for Birmingham'. He noted that the Corporation had promised temporary accommo-dation for a Natural History Museum in the new Municipal Buildings in Edmund Street (1905) and that the Society had undertaken to receive and to hold in trust for the Corporation (at Avebury House in Newhall Street) donations of collections or of single objects until the museum was ready. By 1911 their rooms were quite full and the Corporation had to hire additional rooms in Avebury House. He then went on to outline all that was required for a permanent Natural History Museum including funding, organisation, ac-quisitions policy, environmental control in the galler-ies, staffing, and the arrangement of the collections themselves.

In June 1910 the scheme for a museum was officially adopted by the Corporation and active preparation to achieve it was begun. The Corporation agreed to provide accommodation for the collections and to maintain them, but not to provide exhibits. The Society already held collections and now set up a Committee (including representatives from the Microscopical Union and the Birmingham Field Naturalists' Club) to obtain help and promises in the formation of museum collections.

Between 1910 and 1913 the Committee busied itself sorting out the collections and drawing up plans for their arrangement. In 1912 the Corporation appointed

W. H. Edwards, previously Curator of the Victoria Institute, Worcester, for seventeen years, as Assistant Keeper to be in charge of the Natural History Museum. Professor Gamble had drawn up the original display scheme but Edwards was responsible for making it a practical reality. It was finally opened on 17 July 1913 in galleries adjacent to the Feeney Art Galleries and part of the Council House Extension. The first gallery (now the Pinto Gallery) was largely vacant, awaiting the Beale Memorial Collection. Alderman Charles Beale, an eminent city politician, benefactor and a keen amateur ornithologist, had died in 1912. A subscription had been raised to establish a permanent memorial to him, and this was allocated to the endowment of a University Chair and to the assembling of 'a collection of British birds and their nests, mounted in their natural surroundings, to be placed in cases in the first room of the future Birmingham Natural History Museum . . .' The Beale Memorial Collection was eventually opened in May 1915. The second gallery, or dome, was used for the display of the larger specimens, including 'the hippopotamus, the rhinoceros and the mountain sheep which had been a feature of interest at Aston Hall for many years . . .' The third contained a variety of specimens illustrating British flora and fauna, and the last gallery, at the Great Charles Street end of the building, contained a large collection of British birds loaned to the museum by R. W. Chase in 1912.

The new galleries were certainly well received by the Council. Half of them were fully equipped with 'modern cases in which to display the collections in the latest approved museum method.' In the first few months of opening 'the galleries have been crowded with visitors, thus proving that a public want has been supplied in that direction.' The new galleries included certain specimens brought from Aston Hall (where the collections had been overhauled and catalogued). They came mostly without data, but were useful, after renovation, for filling in gaps until better specimens could be procured. The opening of the new galleries had required a considerable amount of preparing, mounting and labelling. It was noted that, because of lack of time, 'it was found impossible to classify many of the exhibits scientifically, so that the present arrangement must not be looked upon as a permanent one'.

What had been the guiding principles behind the setting up of the first public Natural History Museum in Birmingham? One of the outside influences in achieving this in the first place had been the great stimulus given to the natural sciences by including them in school curricula and by 'the remarkable flood of popular works of natural history' which occurred in the early years of this century. This created the right climate for the establishment of museums where the knowledge obtained from books and in the field may be amplified by the examination of natural objects set up with due regard to scientific classification. There was therefore a strong emphasis on the educational value of a museum from the outset.

Willoughby Ellis recognised that there were two separate parts in any museum: 'The educational services being regarded as an illustration of the general principles of the sciences relating to the Natural History of the whole world rather than a detailed museum of its productions. The study series on the other hand being a dictionary as complete in every detail as possible, with a view to studying or adding to the knowledge of the natural productions of Great Britain and our own district in particular.'

When calls were being made in the late nineteenth century for a museum, it was suggested that it ought to be representative of the flora and fauna of Warwickshire, Staffordshire, Worcestershire and of the Midlands generally. In July 1910 *The Times* exhorted the proposed museum to 'enlist the sentiment of territorial patriotism', pointing out that a local emphasis would appeal to the people of Birmingham and the surrounding countryside from which the specimens would be drawn and that it would also encourage local naturalists because it would form a reference collection upon which they could focus.

Writing at the same time, Sir Ray Lankester also emphasised the 'local' philosophy: 'We may hope that it will not contain the usual unsatisfactory series of badly-stuffed exotic animals, birds and reptiles, and trophies of South Sea Islanders' clubs and spears. It should contain first-rate specimens of the living and extinct fauna of Warwickshire, and specimens of foreign animals carefully selected to compare with them and throw light on them; also local prehistoric and antiquarian specimens, illustrated by comparison with the work of savage and remote races. The excellent suggestion has been made by a contemporary that it should contain specimens of the insect-pests of Warwickshire crops, and it should also exhibit the minerals from which the manufactories of Birmingham draw their metals, and should exhibit the stages of their preparation.'

But this local approach was not favoured by Willoughby Ellis, whose philosophy seems ultimately to have triumphed: 'Before a scheme is undertaken it is necessary firstly to consider the district which the museum is intended to serve, and secondly that the institution should have some definite object or objects to fulfil. Birmingham is one of the principal centres of population in this country, and not only does it require such an institution but it also demands that it shall be a comprehensive one. The purely local character of the museums of many small towns makes them totally inadequate and a much wider range is necessary.'

Apart from a formal educational role, a Natural History Museum was seen as having two other useful functions. The first may be broadly described as increasing the appreciation of Nature: 'The object of a natural history museum should be first to enable and encourage the citizen to take an intelligent interest in the various forms of animal and vegetable life that he may come across in his occasional walks beyond the limits of city streets, and to stimulate the imagination by showing the wonderful diversity of the natural life of the earth . . . The better we know Nature, the better we know ourselves and that, after all, is the supreme wisdom.' Professor Bridge, one of the early advocates of a museum, followed Ruskin in remarking that it is the duty of a museum to manifest to simple people 'the beauty and life of all things and creatures in their perfectedness'. Alfred Hayes, then Secretary of the Birmingham and Midland Institute and a signatory of the 1904 petition, foresaw the museum's greatest importance 'in the counteracting influence which it would exert to the evil effects inseparable from a huge manufacturing centre, where a large proportion of the population was inevitably out of touch with the healthy and humanising agency of nature'. It was hoped that the study of birds and animals would also 'engender a love of wild life, and tend to arrest the spirit of wanton destruction so common to the rural life of today'. *The Times* even wondered if the appreciation of nature might help to stem the exodus from the countryside to the town. To see a natural history museum as being able to reduce the tide of urbanisation might be expecting too much but its other contention, that it might well stimulate 'a taste for country objects and interests among town-dwellers' was more reasonable.

Hayes also drew attention to the second useful function. In 1904 he remarked that much of the 'meaninglessness' in modern architecture was due to the fact the 'the designs were not taken first hand from nature, as in the Middle Ages'. Several writers drew attention to the value of a natural history museum to students of art and design.

If the basic philosophy of the museum was to lead to problems later on, then so was its location within the 'Council House Extension' adjoining the Feeney Art Galleries. Willoughby Ellis, and others who had campaigned for the Museum, always considered that this was a temporary measure until a separate building, administered independently of the Art Gallery, could be found: 'In the new Municipal Buildings in Edmund Street galleries will be reserved for a Natural History Museum as a temporary measure. This is a good point, for surely the permanent housing of a Museum in such a place, bounded on all sides by apartments allocated to other interests, without space for extension, would be a feature calculated to retard if not entirely check the natural expansion and utility of the collections.' The belief among members of the Society was clearly that the Corporation would honour a promise to provide a museum and that it would not remain in the unsatisfactory Edmund Street galleries.

There were certainly plenty of complaints about these galleries. One was that they could be entered only through the Art Gallery. Another was that they 'were not originally intended to be devoted to any such purpose, and consequently they are not so well adapted to the special requirements [of a Natural History Museum] as they might have been'. The galleries had of course been designed for the hanging of drawings, and there was already a degree of hostility arising from their relationship to the art galleries. 'It must be confessed that the accommodation is not all that could be desired. Suggesting as it does that natural history is a mere side show in an exhibition of works of art and craftsmanship, yet it is sufficient to afford an opportunity to local naturalists of showing what may be done even in limited space, and when the educational influence of the exhibition extends, as I feel sure it will in the course of a few years, the desirability of providing a separate building as the home of the museum will come to be recognised by the City Council.'

There is also some suggestion that Whitworth Wallis himself was not very sympathetic to a natural history museum. He had stated in 1904 that the 'system adopted in many towns of placing the art gallery and the natural history museum in the charge of one individual was altogether a mistake'. Interestingly enough, in 1910, Alfred Hayes, still Secretary of the Birmingham and Midland Institute, felt it necessary to write to the *Birmingham Daily Post* refuting 'the impression . . . that the director of the Art Gallery is not wholly in sympathy with the present movement for the establishment of a municipal exhibition of natural history.'

The initiative taken by the Birmingham Natural History Museum Committee, whose members were central figures in the intellectual and scientific life of the city, and the realisation of their prime objective, resulted in an overwhelming spate of gifts from private collectors in all branches of natural history – more than a hundred contributed in each of the first two years (1912-13) of the new museum. The number of gifts diminished during the ensuing war years and yet many of the most significant collections were received in this brief period. The actual quantitative impact of these gifts of entire collections can be judged from the register entry for that of Sir Benjamin Stone which records: 'large quantity of mosses and other botanical specimens, fossils, minerals, shells, corals, etc. from many parts of the world: also jungle fowl and Japanese giant crab in glass cases and several boxes of exotic insects'. The plant specimens alone, exclusive of mosses, are now known to number almost ten thousand. This is not an isolated example although probably more extensive in its range than most.

Part of the Stone collection.

A giant Japanese Crab (the British Edible Crab provides a size comparison).

During the Great War the museum contributed small exhibits on the danger to health caused by the common domestic fly and on insects, birds and animals both useful and harmful in the garden or allotment. In May 1920 the whole of the Beale Memorial Gallery was finally opened. The forty-two cases contained a representative sample of familiar species of British birds. The curator generally used actual settings taken in the field; the swallow's nest, for example, is exhibited in the actual timber-framed gable end of the Worcestershire barn where it was found. None of the specimens were collected within fifteen miles of Birmingham because the bird from this area 'takes on the colouring of its surroundings, and has less of the gaiety and brilliance of plumage than his brethren of the countryside who are clear of the murk and dirt of the manufacturing centre'. It was particularly remarked that examples of black-headed gulls which had been breeding on the Birmingham Sewage Farm were being sought further afield 'partly to avoid disturbance of the local colony and partly to secure birds of more immaculate plumage'.

The museum, as originally envisaged in its temporary accommodation, was now complete and full within ten years of its creation. In 1924 the Feeney Charitable Trustees decided to purchase the extensive R. W. Chase collection of stuffed and mounted birds for the city. It was immediately recognised that the Chase Collection, some of which had been on loan to the museum since 1913, 'will require a considerable amount of space for its adequate display . . . in this connection the urgent need of further museum space may be emphasised, for already many thousands of museum objects are unfortunately hidden away in store, and it is becoming increasingly difficult to accept offers of gifts, particularly when the proviso is made that gifts must be displayed. This lack of accommodation may result in the loss of valuable collections and objects, for collectors will not present treasures which cannot be exhibited to the public.'

Each additional major gift, such as the Whitelock gift of shells in 1925, aroused further calls for the museum's galleries which were already 'full to overflowing', to be extended. Finally, in 1926, Birmingham's proposed Civic Centre scheme based around the Hall of Memory included provision for a new Natural History Museum. In February 1927 the Museum and Art Gallery Committee finally presented their needs for a new natural history museum ideally to be built upon an independent central site. The proposal did not, however, meet with any great enthusiasm in the press. Museums were desirable, but they had to wait their turn. 'The general level of culture in the city will not suffer if the public be left to make shift for a number of years to come with its present galleries – of which it has cause to be proud.'

In 1928, W. H. Edwards, the curator credited with having created the best display of natural history in a provincial museum, retired. He was a man of retiring nature and devoted to his work, 'but it was very largely due to his capacity for making friends and for inspiring confidence, that the expansion of the natural history collections of the city have far outrun the development of the accommodation for their display'. He was succeeded by Donald Payler who had for seventeen years been Assistant Curator of the Norwich Castle Museum.

Generous gifts continued to come in. At the end of 1928 Alderman Sir George Kenrick presented to the museum his entire library of works on entomology, comprising some five hundred volumes. He had since 1912 made other gifts of 'Midland Coleoptera' (the Blatch Collection, 1912), four cases illustrating the 'Evolution of Lepidoptera' (1915) and his collection of butterflies and moths (1927) not yet housed in the museum because of lack of space, but eventually received and accommodated in 1932. In the same year the Reverend P. G. M. Rhodes, of Oscott College (who had been associated with the museum before), 'presented his fine collection of British and foreign lichens, comprising nearly three thousand named specimens. However his larger collection of mosses (10,000 specimens) he donated shortly before his death (1934) to the British Museum in London. His certain knowledge of the dire shortage of space in Birmingham's natural history museum may have influenced that decision, for he had already earned official thanks for his voluntary assistance in identifying and naming mosses, hepatics and lichens in the department's plant collections. Included among the

The museum's ethnographical collections were first displayed and curated by the Natural History department.

British specimens are many collected in the Birmingham district and during the recent survey of
Hartlebury Common. These are especially valuable, as
the lichen flora of the Midlands is rapidly diminishing.'
Kenrick and Rhodes were just two of a long list of
members of the Birmingham Natural History and
Philosophical Society whose gifts formed the foundation collections in natural history at Birmingham
Museum.

Donald Payler organised a number of small temporary exhibitions, including a series of 'economic
exhibits' dealing with such topics as insect pests and
the 'commercial utility of common substances' often
based on raw materials used in Birmingham industries.
In 1929 he instituted seasonal Nature Study Exhibits;
these consisted of changing displays (weekly) from
April to October of wild flowers, the success of which
'is due to the remarkable enthusiasm shown by the
many ladies and gentlemen responsible for providing
the exhibits.'

There were extensive re-arrangements of the galleries
in 1929 and 1930 which aroused some hostile criticism.
One correspondent to the *Birmingham Daily Post*
enquired as to what 'evil genius has been let loose to
destroy the artistic charm' of the museum, leaving one
only to be impressed by the 'methodical arrangement
of exhibits, labelled as in a saleroom'. Among the
casualties of the new arrangements were the rhinoceros
and hippopotamus from Aston Hall, declared 'bad
specimens of their kind and unworthy of a first-class
Natural History Museum'. These re-arrangements
allowed the opening in 1931 of two new sections
devoted to Ethnography and Prehistory. The disposal
of the Feeney collection of casts of classical sculptures
released two further galleries for the developing
department of antiquities and for the creation of
geological displays including fossils and minerals in
1933. At the same time it was possible to devote one
gallery to 'biological exhibits of an economic nature'.
Many related to Birmingham industries, dealing with
the manufacturing processes involved in the preparation of tortoiseshell, ivory, bone, lac, rubber and other
commodities. But there were also practical exhibits
relating to timber diseases, tree pruning and garden
pests.

The Natural History collections at
Aston Hall.

The late 1930s was apparently a quiet period of
consolidation with little in the way of innovation.
Nevertheless, twenty years of collection building
and gallery interpretation of a high standard had
established Birmingham Museum's Natural History
Department among the best. The new labelling and
display methods introduced by Payler were a reflection
of the growing professionalism among museum
curators in the 1930s. Specimens were to fulfil a
particular purpose in the galleries and not simply to
remain there because they were 'old favourites'. The
galleries themselves were to be re-arranged to better
reflect the changing expectations of visitors. But while
change in the galleries was one way in which curators
such as Payler could ensure vitality in the museum, the
role of the Keeper was still very important in 'setting
the tone' of the Museum and Art Gallery.

Between the Wars

The appointment of a new Keeper in May 1927 heralded in a new era for the Museum and Art Gallery. S. C. Kaines Smith came from Leeds Art Gallery of which he was Director. He had previously studied archaeology in Greece and was well known as a writer on art and as a lecturer, having been the first to give official guide-lectures at the National Gallery. He has been described as having a 'colossal personality' which certainly dominated the years between Sir Whitworth's death and the Second World War. He put a tremendous amount of effort into exhorting Birmingham citizens to contribute to the Art Gallery in any way in which they could. Through his willingness to enter into controversy he kept the Art Gallery in the news. Add to this the series of successful exhibitions which he organised and he was able to give the Museum a 'higher public profile' than it had enjoyed for many years previously.

Kaines Smith clearly despaired of the Birmingham public from time to time. He often seems to have viewed the Art Gallery as an oasis of culture in a city which did not deserve it. In May 1931, for example, he opened an address to the Birmingham Rotary Club with a favourite theme of his: 'Like all Birmingham people, you are, I suppose, very proud of the Museum and Art Gallery, and like all good Birmingham citizens, you never go inside!' He went on to a second favourite theme: that not one item in the collections had been paid for out of the local rates. He was in favour of its remaining that way, associating Purchase Funds from the rates with interference from Councillors: 'It is not that I don't want the money, but can you imagine the kind of picture that the majority of the members of a committee would purchase?'

Nevertheless the reliance on private donors to provide funds for major acquisitions undoubtedly brought its own problems, not least of them the lack of such funds. But Kaines Smith stuck to his theme and his criticism of the lack of generosity of Birmingham people. At a meeting of the Birmingham and Edgbaston Debating Society in February 1934 he said that: 'In Birmingham I can count 1200 people in three generations who have made the Art Gallery what it is, and yet the rest of the people, who have given nothing,

say they are proud of it'. In March 1935 Kaines Smith had a letter published in the *Birmingham Post* which acknowledged the decision of Leslie Barnwell to donate two pictures (which had been on loan for some time) to mark the Silver Jubilee of King George V. Barnwell had commented: 'I feel that, if others who have in a similar way made loans to the Gallery could be induced to do likewise, the Gallery might be the richer by a great many interesting and important works; and that this would be a very fitting form of celebration this year'. Kaines Smith took up this call with enthusiasm. He remarked that if everyone did as Mr Barnwell suggested: 'not only would our collections be very greatly enriched, but we should be relieved of the constantly haunting danger of losing some of the most interesting exhibits at present in the Gallery. I think that, if the general public realised to what an extent they are indebted to the lenders as well as to the donors of works of art, they would appreciate how much room there is for additions to the permanent collection . . . Although the pride of Birmingham in its Art Gallery is

Some items were donated to Birmingham by the artist; Frank Brangwyn's *Workman with Pickaxe* (1931) is an example.

Valentine Lefèbre, *Landscape with Love and Psyche*, donated in 1930.

The Friends of the Museum and Art Gallery presented this William Morris design for *Jasmine* (1872) in 1941.

constantly expressed, an analysis of gifts of funds in recent years would reveal the fact that surprisingly few of Birmingham's citizens have real cause for this pride. Their attitude should rather be that of gratitude to the comparatively few who have made the Art Gallery what it is. The generosity of the past has produced a splendid collection; and unless it is now to stand still − which is tantamount to going backwards − the circle of supporters of the Gallery must be widened. This is surely the best possible moment at which to embark upon that enterprise.'

It had been concern about lack of support for purchases which had prompted the foundation of an 'Association of the Friends of the Gallery' in March 1931. In a pamphlet launching the Association Kaines Smith had noted that over the last three years £11,550 had been contributed for purchases by only 14 individuals. The Association had been formed so that large numbers of people could contribute an annual subscription which would form an annual income into a purchase fund. Thus the Art Gallery would no longer be dependent on the limited circle of those to whom an individual appeal could be made in an emergency.

The Association was constituted in July 1931 and the first three purchases were made. The first was a flower study in oil, *Cyclamen*, by the Birmingham artist Mrs Florence Engelbach (who was the wife of C. F. F. Engelbach, Works Director of the Austin Motor Company). The second was a seventeenth-century miniature by Mumtaz Mahal, in whose memory Shah Jehan built the Taj Mahal at Agra. The third picture was a mid-nineteenth-century cameo by Schmidt. It was the beginning of a vital contribution to the success of the Art Gallery in the past fifty years.

Kaines Smith's years as Keeper certainly saw the steady increase in the collections of all departments, though with relatively few spectacular additions. Sir Charles Hyde (Feeney's nephew and his successor as proprietor of the *Birmingham Post*) donated *The Distressed Poet* by William Hogarth and other notable paintings were acquired, mainly by British artists. In 1927 J. R. Holliday bequeathed a large collection of Pre-Raphaelite and Cox drawings, while significant groups of drawings relating to A. J. Gaskin, Frank Brangwyn and the Canziani family followed. There were some important additions to the ceramic collections. Hyde's tsuba collection, the Barnett bequest of rings and the substantial Greenberg gift of silver consolidated the quality of the metalwork collections.

It was perhaps more for what he did with the collections than for what was acquired during his Keepership that Kaines Smith should be remembered. He has perhaps tended to be forgotten in Birmingham, squeezed as he is between the prodigious Wallis and the much-loved Trenchard Cox. Yet it was he who may be credited with creating a Museum Service out of an Art Collection, or at least with starting that process.

One area of the collections which Kaines Smith was keen to expand was that of contemporary art. He, in many ways, carried forward the original concept of a Museum and Art Gallery influencing the community which it served. He believed that art was fundamentally important to the development of both industry and town planning, not least of all in Birmingham. He once said that the first step towards an artistic renaissance in Birmingham should be a serious and concerted effort to make Birmingham itself a beautiful city, and praised some of the suburban developments of the early 1930s. He also recognised the need to educate the people of Birmingham with regard to the City's own contribution in the past to those decorative arts which were so important to the silversmith, jeweller and other Birmingham craftsmen. He felt strongly that the 'art industry' could transform the quality of mass-produced items, and that the Museum had its part to play, although '... the vast majority of work produced and sold has no individuality whatever, and is merely a vain repetition of the ghost of an old fashion, or, if it aims at originality, arrives only at eccentricity'.

Tissot's *Study of a Girl* (1869) was part of the important J. R. Holliday Bequest of 1927.

Eighteenth-century Worcester porcelain,
donated by various individuals 1907-1926.

Kaines Smith was here prepared to confront what he
saw as important contemporary issues in Birmingham
which were relevant to his role as Director of the
Museum and Art Gallery. But he did recognise his own
limitations: 'It is not for me to solve this problem. It is
only for me to remind Birmingham people that the best
Birmingham craftsmen are here, are available, and that
their work bears no trace of eccentricity whatever. It
has a fine usefulness as its primary characteristic of the
Birmingham designer in all the crafts. He has produced
an article which will do the job, and there have always
been individual craftsmen who have produced such
things as if they loved their jobs. And that, after all, is
art.'

He backed up his exhortations to persuade designers
and manufacturers to produce cheap beautiful things
rather than ugly ones by staging exhibitions to encourage them in this direction. In 1934 he organised a
'Midland Industrial Art Exhibition' comprising a wide

range of artistically-designed objects produced on a commercial basis for daily use. He included the work only of firms in the eleven counties within a fifty-mile radius of Birmingham, but collaborated closely with the Design & Industries Association who later repeated the idea in London. The announcement of the exhibition coincided with the first meeting of the newly-formed Council for Art and Industry, and therefore received much national attention. Kaines Smith appeared on a round-table discussion on art and the manufacturer which was broadcast on the Midland Home Service. It was all a major success in bringing Birmingham into the limelight. This was followed by two further major 'blockbuster' exhibitions, 'Art Treasures of the Midlands' (also in 1934) and 'Heraldic Art' in 1936, the largest exhibition of its kind ever held in Britain.

The years of Kaines Smith's keepership included a broadening and reorganisation of the subject matter on display in the Museum. The whole Museum underwent re-labelling and a rationalisation of objects on display, but with major changes in the Great Charles Street suite of galleries. When opened in 1919 two galleries had been devoted to displaying the 'Museum of Casts'. The casts were designed to give the student a knowledge of the development of Greek and Roman sculpture from the sixth century BC to AD 114. 'Although of undoubted use to a small number of students, this valuable collection of casts was not found to be fulfilling the educational purpose for which it had been primarily intended'. Consequently the Feeney Charitable Trustees gave their permission for the dispersal of the collection (mainly to Perth Museum and Art Gallery) and it was removed.

This caused quite a stir. Some described it as 'an act of vandalism' and one, when informed of what was to replace the casts, commented that 'It cannot be imagined that stuffed birds, dead animals, and cast-off clothing of a generation or two ago are to compensate for their loss'. Others welcomed the action as 'being another step in the direction of brightening and making more interesting the Art Gallery from the point of view of the merely interested and general visitor'. Kaines Smith himself could not be drawn to make any comment and the *Birmingham Gazette* reporter sent to interview him had to rely upon the amusement that the 'nude casts' gave to the young and 'the embarrassment which I feel sure gripped most males'. All that remains now is the classical frieze around the West Midlands Archaeology Gallery.

The removal of the 'Museum of Casts' was an essential preliminary to the opening of the Archaeology and Textiles Galleries in its place in 1933. The latter consisted of collections of costumes, woven fabrics, embroideries, lace and ecclesiastical vestments which had been rapidly increasing during the previous few years. The core of the new gallery was a miscellaneous collection of eighteenth- and nineteeth-century British costume.

The early years of Whitworth Wallis's keepership had seen Greek and Roman antiquities among the gifts to the Museum, but interest in these collections seems to have evaporated by the Great War. After the war there were a few important additions. The Paul Ellis collection of classical jewellery in gold and silver was presented by the Birmingham Association of Jewellers in 1920, supplemented by the Barnett collection in 1935. Also in the 1930s Sir Charles Hyde subscribed financial funds to the excavation of the neolithic tell at Vinca, near Belgrade, and in return the excavator presented the Museum with a major collection of antiquities. A similar arrangement also involving Hyde led to the acquisition of material from excavations at Nineveh in Palestine. This reliance on private funding in order to secure collections obviously meant a loss of curatorial control on acquisitions. The British collections consisted of only a few boxes of prehistoric stone implements and medieval pottery from Weoley Castle. No sponsor interested in Midland archaeology had come forward to rectify this failing.

In November 1932 Theodore Burton Brown, an archaeologist who had taken part in excavations at Jericho, was appointed Junior Assistant Keeper. Less than twelve months later the new Archaeology Gallery was opened, but not all the archaeological collections could yet be brought together. The Department of Natural History had been acquiring prehistoric and ethnographical items during the 1920s (including the major collection of Pacific Ethnography donated by A. W. Wilkins) and had opened sections within its own

Ivories from Nineveh.

The A. W. Wilkins collection of Ethnography.

galleries devoted to these subjects in 1931. Nicholas Thomas has identified the lack of a purchase fund and the absence of an Archaeology department as the reasons for the slow and perhaps eccentric growth of archaeological and ethnographical collections before the Second World War. Nonetheless the 1930s did see some positive advance and the establishment of Birmingham's world-wide antiquities collecting policy, in itself crucial to understanding the nature of archaeology in Birmingham Museum today.

The expansion of the archaeology and the natural history collections was sufficient in the 1930s to lead to a suggestion, in 1939, that an entirely new museum should be built as part of a proposed Civic Centre development. The space released in the Feeney Galleries could then be used for the display of prints and drawings. However the intervention of war put an end to this idea and the Museum and Art Gallery were to remain as sometimes uncomfortable bedfellows.

Although the re-organisation of the Central Museum

Local prints and drawings in the museum's collection are a fine visual source for Birmingham history.

The Birmingham Historical Museum, Cannon Hill.

and Art Gallery was important, it is in the promotion of 'branch museums' that Kaines Smith may be best honoured. In 1927 there was only one 'branch' of the Central Museum, Aston Hall, and this was a rather special case. By the end of the 1930s another three had been added and the concept of 'suburban museums' was established.

The history of the museum at Cannon Hill is a curious one. Kaines Smith originally intended to establish a series of suburban Art Galleries of which Cannon Hill was to be the first. Its building was authorised as such in 1929 and when a competition for designs was arranged (the winner was selected from thirty-three entries) it was described (and designed) as a 'Branch Art Gallery'. But between then and its opening in 1931 a change of purpose came about. In 1927 the hope had been expressed that a 'Birmingham Historical Museum' might be established on a central site: 'Nothing has occurred since then to alter this point of view, but the growing necessity for branch galleries similar to those already established in Manchester and other large cities, has been impressed upon your Committee by a variety of circumstances; and simul-

Bell Street in 1830. A glimpse
of a piece of Birmingham long since
destroyed but recreated by the Museum's
collections.

taneously, the growth of the collections pertaining to
the history of Birmingham has been considerable,
many gifts having been made or promised on the
understanding that serious effort would be made to
exhibit them in an historical group at the earliest
possible date. Your Committee therefore feels that the
erection of a building of the kind indicated in Cannon
Hill Park would serve in the first instance to redeem
the promises of early exhibition of objects of historical
interest to Birmingham, and that when eventually a
central site could be found for a Birmingham Historical
Museum, the building in question could take up its
proper function of a branch Art Gallery'. And so the
Birmingham Historical Museum was created. Later it
became a Natural History Museum but it never did
'take up its proper function'.

When the museum opened in 1931 it contained
items illustrating many aspects of the civic, political,
religious, educational and topographical history of the
city. It was the nucleus of a collection. There were
various 'local views', many by members of the Lines
family, an 'Ecclesiastical and Educational' case
(consisting almost entirely of tokens and medals), a

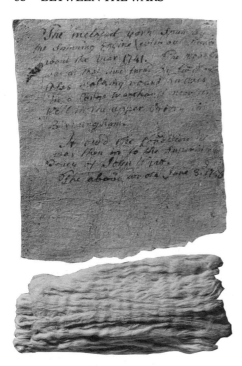

The world's first hank of cotton, spun in Birmingham in 1741.

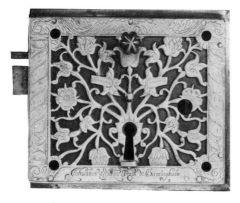

The John Wilkes lock, a fine example of seventeenth-century Birmingham craftsmanship.

case of medals, a case of tokens, two cases mainly of material relating to firefighting (on loan from the Birmingham Fire Brigade), a case of objects associated with Birmingham 'worthies', and a 'Science and Industry' case (very inadequate). Finally there were five cases devoted to Birmingham industries covering silver, jewellery, glass, papier-mâché and tortoiseshell. Many of the items had been acquired before 1890 (much of the jewellery, for example, was acquired in 1887), but there had also been a marked increase in acquisitions from 1927 onwards. All the displays included a number of loans, often greater than the permanent collection.

Although the numismatic collections were already academically important, many of the other local history artefacts were a mixture of 'curiosities' and the beginnings of important representative collections. In 1886 a Mrs Silvester had donated 'The first Hank of Cotton spun by machinery', while in 1892 four silver coins and newspapers were collected 'from the Weather-cock on Aston Church'. On the other hand the button and cut steel collections were already begun; in 1893 the Lines family drawings were acquired which laid the foundation of a local prints and drawings collection; and, finally, there were individual items of importance such as the seventeenth-century lock by John Wilkes.

Nevertheless, a *Staffordshire Advertiser* reporter identified its shortcomings. He stated: 'it is certain that if Birmingham is to make its historical museum relative to local developments and progress fully representative, a building six times as large as the new building will be required to accommodate the features of interest . . . The probability, however, is that so many valuable exhibits of local history interest will be retained at the Art Gallery and Museum in the city, that the Cannon Hill institution will be little more than an overflow for articles for which no room could be found elsewhere'. And so it proved. Interest in the museum waned and it was finally decided to turn it over to the Natural History Department in 1955. It remained as a Natural History Museum until 1977 by which time it had been superseded by the Nature Centre developed on an adjacent site.

The second venture was Highbury, a branch museum which was unsought and has been until recently largely unloved. Highbury was built in 1879 to the design of

Highbury, the home of Joseph Chamberlain.

John Henry Chamberlain, Birmingham's leading architect, and set in substantial grounds. It was the home of Joseph Chamberlain from then until his death in 1914. His library and study, which looks out on to the gardens, is lined with elaborately carved bookcases and a marquetry ceiling of walnut, elm and sycamore has a design of horse-chestnuts and ivy-leaves. This room was 'the scene of many important gatherings in the memorable days of the organisation of the Liberal Associations, the Home Rule split, the formation of the Unionist party, when great statesmen as well as leaders of thought in Birmingham met Mr Joseph Chamberlain to discuss the trend of events and the action to be taken. Here, indeed, much history was made.'

In 1914 Highbury was inherited by Austen Chamberlain who placed the house and grounds at the disposal of a Voluntary Aid Detachment for use as an annexe to the First Southern General Hospital at the University buildings in Edgbaston. In 1919 Sir Austen

'Jimmy the Rockman', a Birmingham character immortalised in this brass relief.

gave the house to the Highbury trustees and the buildings were used as a hospital for disabled servicemen until 1932. In that year the trustees presented Highbury to Birmingham Corporation and it was opened as a Home for Aged Women.

The Museum and Art Gallery Committee were made responsible for setting up the library at Highbury as a museum and, with the generous donations of members of the Chamberlain family and the public, assembled a collection of Chamberlain memorabilia. These items ranged from a collection of addresses presented to him by numerous public bodies, original political cartoons and portraits in a variety of media to small personal items such as his monocle and his meerschaum pipe which was donated by the son of a former head gardener at Highbury. The majority of these items were displayed in glass-fronted cases formed from the original built-in bookcases after the removal of the shelves. Progress on forming this 'Chamberlain Museum' was hampered by the fact that the majority of Joseph's books had been incorporated into Sir Austen's library and the furniture had been sold at auction in London without its being disclosed that it belonged to Chamberlain. Thus it was difficult to re-assemble authentic material. Nevertheless, the 'Joseph Chamberlain Memorial Museum' was opened on 9 July 1934.

Five years later, on the outbreak of war the museum was closed 'for the duration' and was not re-opened until 30 November 1949. Unfortunately by the mid-1950s attendance figures had dwindled, and although the Museum and Art Gallery had proposed extending the Chamberlain Museum these plans did not material-ise, so that by May 1962 it had become a room for the elderly residents to receive their visitors, though people interested in seeing the museum were admitted by appointment. In 1981 the Chamberlain personalia was brought back to the City Museum, and, early in 1984, work started on a renovation programme at the house in order that it might be used as a civic conference and reception centre. These plans (at the time of writing) include the refurbishment of Joseph Chamberlain's library and the provision of a new interpretation room.

Blakesley Hall (in the parish of Yardley) was the third new branch museum developed during the Keepership of Kaines Smith. One of the finest surviving timber-framed buildings within the city boundary, it was built shortly after 1573 by Richard Smalbroke, a Birmingham merchant. The house passed by marriage to the Foliot family, by whom it was sold in 1685. For the next two hundred years it was occupied by various tenant farmers, but by the late nineteenth century it was largely used as an attractive home for a series of Birmingham businessmen. In 1901 it was bought by Thomas Merry, a local paint and varnish manufacturer.

Merry died in 1932 and the property was eventually offered to the Corporation for £3000. In response to an appeal the Common Good Trust offered to loan the sum to the City Council, interest-free for twelve months, to allow them to purchase the Hall. They then had to decide what to do with it. 'The proposal favoured by the General Purposes Committee is that the building should be formed into a branch museum, on the lines of the highly-successful Didsbury Museum in Manchester, whose surroundings are of a similar character to those of Blakesley Hall, attached to which there are large gardens and more than five acres of ground. These amenities, it was agreed, could be utilised for purposes of recreation.' Thus it became Kaines Smith's responsibility, which was appropriate because he had taken a leading part in the appeal to save it, even if he did not seem to have any clear idea what to do with it.

Little was known about the Hall. In 1935 the first guide book insisted that 'the history of Blakesley Hall, which can never have been more than a typical dwelling house of comparatively small importance, is to all intents and purposes beyond recovery'. There was therefore no intention to present the Hall as a furnished historic house. When it opened in 1935 its role was defined as being 'a repository of all obtainable information with regard to the history of the medieval manors on whose ground the modern city of Birmingham stands'. The displays consisted of photographs of the ancient buildings and landmarks of the city while elsewhere the boundaries, manorial descents, and shields showing the armorial bearings of each of Birmingham's manors were presented. Each shield was hand-painted by Kaines Smith, who was a recognised expert in heraldry.

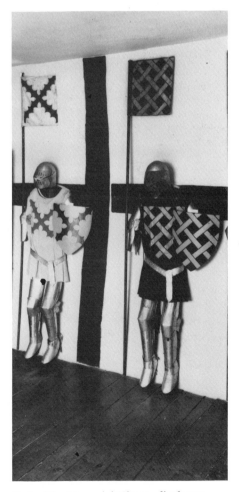

Part of the Manorial History display at Blakesley Hall, 1950.

These sparse displays remained intact until the war. In November 1941 a bomb fell on the north side of the house causing extensive external and internal damage. The Hall remained semi-derelict for some years. In 1943 it was recorded that the Director hoped to remove the old manorial displays at the Hall and arrange additional exhibits to deal with social history and culture prior to the Industrial Revolution. But the Museum did not re-open until 1957 by which time it was the responsibility of the Department of Archaeology. Although 'a modicum of furniture' was 'employed to lend atmosphere', it was still primarily a traditional local history museum. One room described in painful detail the excavation of a Roman site at Mancetter, setting out 'the whole process of digging and deduction . . . with the hope that the layman will be able to see how it is done'. Other rooms contained displays on several of Birmingham's past industries, of local costume and an attempt to illustrate the town's history from the Middle Ages onwards. Finally another room was given over to a vast scale model of Birmingham in 1731.

This was all very well, but it did not satisfy the need for a centrally-located Local History Gallery to tell the story of the city. Nor did it tell the visitor much about Blakesley. In the 1970s Stephen Price set about researching the Hall's history. Sufficient documentation was uncovered to make it feasible to re-display the Hall in harmony with its own history. Rooms are now being re-furnished according to an inventory of 1684 while the interpretative displays concentrate on the history of Blakesley and Yardley. The Hall is now an 'authentic' period house as well as an important environmental studies resource for school classes examining the relationship between environment and social history in its widest sense.

None of the branch museums have ended up quite as Kaines Smith envisaged. But the credit due to him should not be less for this fact. In a few years he immeasurably expanded the service potential of Birmingham Museum and Art Gallery. Indeed, his whole Keepership broadened horizons. It may be argued that, despite his idiosyncratic approach to museums, he can lay claim to being the first of the 'modern' professional curators.

Modern Times

At the outbreak of the Second World War the Museum and Art Gallery was closed and the collections were sent to a number of 'safe' locations in the country. Kaines Smith retired in 1941 and A. E. Whitley became Acting Keeper until the appointment of Mr Trenchard Cox to the post of Director in 1944. Cox had been educated at Eton and Cambridge and had studied the History of Art in Paris and Berlin. He had worked at the National Gallery, the British Museum, the Royal Academy and finally the Wallace Collection prior to coming to Birmingham.

The twenty years of Cox's Directorship and that of his successor, Mary Woodall, were to see a number of major changes and successes. During this time the art collections were broadened in their scope, the archaeology collections grew in importance and the Science Museum was founded. It was also a period of expansion in terms of staffing and of the functions undertaken by the museum service.

The first change was an administrative one, intended to bring the museum into line with the National museums. The Museum and Art Gallery was divided into three Departments (Paintings, Natural History and Archaeology) each under the charge of a Keeper who referred to the Director in matters of policy. At the end of 1945 the three Keepers were Dr Mary Woodall (Paintings), W. A. Seaby (Archaeology) and D. Payler (Natural History). Mr Seaby was succeeded by Adrian

This J. M. W. Turner drawing was included in the J. Leslie Wright Bequest of 1953.

Gustave Doré's *La Marseillaise* was donated by Sir John Holder in 1884, an unusually early gift of a foreign drawing.

Oswald in 1950, in which year the post of Administrator was created, the first holder being Keith Lamb.

There was another important change at the beginning of Trenchard Cox's Directorship. Since the Art Gallery's foundation it had generally been forced to rely on the generosity of individuals and the resources of a few private funds and trusts in the building up of its collections. In 1945 the City Council agreed to provide £1000 annually for the purchase of works of art and specimens for the Museum and Art Gallery. This was increased to £5000 two years later. It was this change in Corporation policy which helped post-war curators to develop the art collections in new directions.

The post-1945 period saw a major change in emphasis in the collection of paintings. Prior to the Second World War the collections were almost exclusively British. Only one significant Old Master (i.e. non-British) painting was presented to the Art Gallery in the nineteenth century to which was added a handful

Canaletto's *Warwick Castle*, one of two views purchased after a major fund-raising campaign in 1978.

purchased by the PPGF in the 1930s. Much more typical of the PPGF's contribution was its first acquisition, Lord Leighton's *A Condottière*. The Art Gallery Purchase Fund acquisitions and private donations were all British. By 1939 the collection was the product of buying contemporary British Art as it appeared, with pictures painted in the early nineteenth century or earlier added by chance of gifts. It was characterised by contemporary British painting, the Pre-Raphaelite collection and the works of two Birmingham artists, Sir Edward Coley Burne-Jones and David Cox.

The creation of a major Old Master Collection (particularly strong in seventeeth-century Italian paintings) is the achievement of the years since 1945 when the efforts of the PPGF were supplemented by the creation of the growing annual purchase grant within the Museum's budget. This introduced a strong element of direction from professional curators to counterbalance the historically dominant element of gifted acquisition.

Two recent examples may be noted to illustrate how important the various sources of funding have now become to collection-building in the art field. In 1978 two 'portraits' of Warwick Castle painted by Canaletto

Rubens's sketch of *James I Uniting England and Scotland* purchased in 1984 by drawing on support from a number of different sources.

for the owners of the castle in the mid-eighteenth century were purchased. These, having strong local interest as well as obvious attractions as works of art, were rescued from export by a major appeal to which gallery visitors, Friends of the Museum, industry, commerce, charitable trusts and the West Midlands County Council responded as well as Government-funded grant-making bodies.

Secondly, in 1984 an oil sketch rather than a finished picture (in itself a relatively new element in the methods by which the collection grows) of *James I Uniting England and Scotland* by Rubens was purchased by drawing on a number of sources. The City of Birmingham made a special capital grant which was supplemented by substantial grants from the National Art Collections Fund and the Victoria and Albert Museum which administers funds from Central Government. However, two-thirds of the total required came from the National Heritage Memorial Fund in

Mrs Martyn by Allan Ramsay was purchased in 1957.

recognition of the historical as well as aesthetic importance of the painting, which is one of only three
Rubens sketches for the ceiling of Charles I's Ban-
queting House at Whitehall still in the country: the
other twelve are abroad. The sale price itself was
dramatically less than the open market valuation
thanks to existing tax concessions for vendors who sell
to a public museum.

As has been outlined, but for the post-Second-
World-War policy of following an international brief,
the character of the Birmingham paintings collection
would be exclusively British. However, since 1945
there have also been changes in the collecting policy
with regard to the British collections. Purchases of
paintings by Richard Wilson, Allan Ramsay and
Thomas Gainsborough have pushed the collection
back into the century during which a strong native
school of painting was established. Although there are
still several large gaps in the seventeenth-century

Peter Lely's *Oliver Cromwell*.

(right) Willem Van de Velde the Younger, *The Hampton Court,* an example of the work of one of the important immigrant artists to England in the late seventeenth century.

collection, two important immigrant artists, Sir Peter Lely and Willem Van de Velde the Younger, are represented.

The nineteenth-century British collection has not been so much of a concern since the War because of its existing relative strength, but at least three major earlier-nineteenth-century paintings, by Landseer, Wilkie and Eastlake, were added in the 1950s. The twentieth-century collections are almost exclusively British and are dominated by two factors. The first is a revival of the original policy to acquire contemporary work, by which means paintings by Bacon, Nicholson and Vaughan have been added to the collection. The other factor has been the representation of artists trained at the Birmingham School of Art, a major centre of art education in the twenty years on either side of 1900. Joseph Southall, Arthur Gaskin, Henry Payne and others are now represented by several works which give the Birmingham Collection a distinct flavour. Joseph Southall, who was a major figure in the revival of tempera painting, painted murals in the Council House and one of the principal staircases of the Museum itself. He and others of this group have been the subject of a series of exhibitions and publications by George Breeze, Glennys Wild and Stephen Wildman, representing a substantial contribution to scholarship.

Richard Wilson's *Okehampton Castle*,
purchased in 1948 to help broaden
Birmingham's British paintings collection.

Edward Landseer's *The Hunting of Chevy
Chase* was presented by the National Art
Collections Fund in 1952.

Modern prints continue to be added to the collections. David Hockney's *Portrait of Man Ray* was given by the Friends of the Museum and Art Gallery in 1979.

(right) Keith Vaughan's *Harvest Assembly* (presented by the Friends of the Museum and Art Gallery in 1963) represents the revived policy of acquiring contemporary work.

Henry Payne was a prominent member of the 'Birmingham School'. This is his *The Choosing of the Red and White Roses* (1908).

(opposite) Joseph Southall's tempera painting in the Art Gallery. The man on the far right is Whitworth Wallis.

CORPORATION STREET BIRMINGHAM
IN MARCH 1914

Epstein's *Lucifer*.

The sculpture collection parallels the paintings in its development. A large amount of architectural sculpture was acquired in the early days, perhaps consciously following the model of the Victoria and Albert Museum in London. Although the *Virgin and Child* out of Andrea Verrochio's workshop was acquired in 1895 the 'Old Master' sculpture collection also dates from the post-1945 period. Also since the Second World War the work of contemporary British sculptors has been added to the collection, including such major figures as Henry Moore, Barbara Hepworth and Jacob Epstein, whose *Lucifer* is one of the Museum's major exhibits.

Other major areas have undergone spectacular growth in the post-1945 period, though the areas of growth have often been determined by the pre-1900 'foundation' collections. Greek and Roman antiquities were an important element in these early collections but it was not until after 1950 that archaeological material became a significant part of the Museum's collections. This unprecedented growth of the archaeological collections was drawn from a wide variety of sources and it was itself so varied that the worldwide character of the collections was firmly established. Much of the material, however, came from early excavations, was undocumented, and therefore of relatively little scholarly value. In 1951 Birmingham began providing funds for the support of excavations at home and abroad, from which in return the City would receive archaeological artefacts from properly conducted excavations. In the years which followed, major collections from the Middle East in particular were acquired by this means. At the same time other material was purchased as a result of the new Purchase Grant arrangement.

The numismatic collections display a similar history. Coins and medals have always been an important part of Birmingham's collections. Foundation gifts from the earliest days of the Museum's existence include those of William Staunton (a large collection of local medals and tokens purchased in 1875), Walter Scott (a collection of ancient coins donated in 1877) and Allan Preston (Soho coins and medals presented in 1878). Under the curatorial influence of Antony Gunstone and his successors other major collections have been

Athenian neck-handled amphora of *c.*525 B C.

The Birmingham Mint's products form an important part of the numismatic collections.

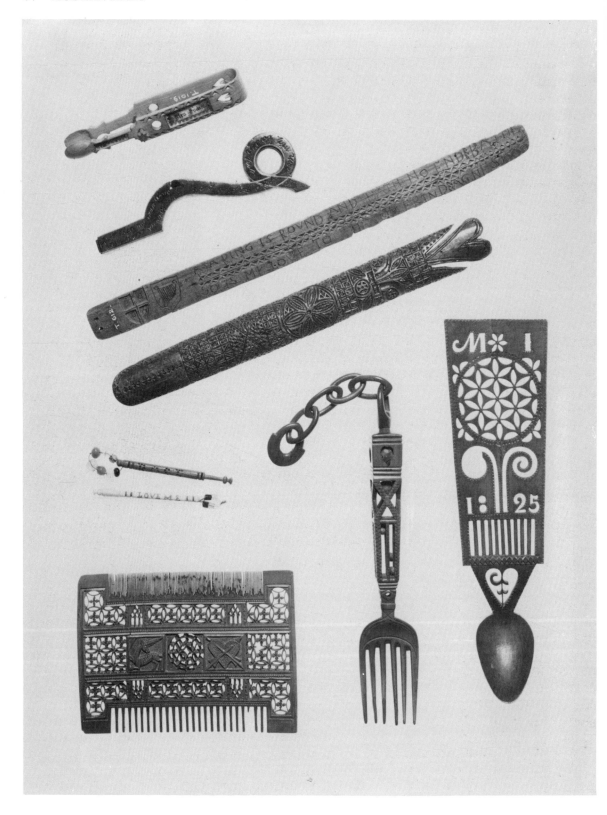

added in recent years. Two were once again purchases partly facilitated by the availability of a Purchase Grant. These were the C. W. Peck collection of George III base metal coins in 1969 and the Birmingham Mint collection in 1981. Finally, the Wellcome Institute collection of Greek and Roman coins was donated in 1981 as part of a much greater gift of archaeological artefacts.

One pillar of curatorial collecting policies has always been 'filling gaps'. Usually this is achieved by a slow process but occasionally one gift or purchase can transform the situation. In 1965 a collection of silver formed by Frederick du Cane Godman (1834-1919) was presented to the Museum by his daughter. Continental silver forms the greater part of the Godman Collection. Prior to 1965 Birmingham had few continental pieces, the first of which were donated by John Feeney who acquired a sizeable collection of jewellery, enamels and silver on his travels to the continent. The most important pieces given to the Museum by Feeney were Scandinavian. In addition to his gift the Museum made several purchases in the 1880s and 1890s but thereafter there was little until the Godman Collection came along.

An example of a 'collector's collection' acquired by the Museum is the Pinto Collection. Edward Pinto had started his collection of treen in the 1920s when he was impressed by the fine craftsmanship and design of many wooden objects. After his marriage to Eva, they both devoted much time to the collection which grew rapidly. Along with it grew their expertise and pre-eminent knowledge of treen. In 1954 they decided to turn the entire lower floor of their residence in Northwood, Middlesex, into a museum. This was a great success; too much, in fact, because with failing health the Pintos could not meet the demands upon them. In 1966, therefore, they appealed for a public museum to offer to acquire their world-famous collection at a nominal purchase price. Birmingham secured it with a telephone call while a rival museum's application was delayed by a national postal strike. The Pinto Gallery was opened to the public in 1969.

As far as the galleries were concerned, the first priority at the end of the Second World War had, of course, to be simply to get the Museum and Art Gallery

Nutcracker from the Pinto Collection.

(opposite) A selection of items from the Pinto Collection.

The Pinto Gallery, as opened in 1969.

open again. Six of the Feeney Galleries were re-opened in 1944-5, but it was not until 1950 that all the undamaged galleries were finally vacated by their wartime occupants and returned to museum use. There remained those galleries which had been damaged in 1940 when a parachute mine had torn down part of the façade of the Council House Extension.

Unfortunately it was not until towards the end of 1955 that reconstruction work began on the bomb-damaged galleries, even though their restoration had been 'under consideration' since 1949. The opportunity was taken to introduce modern facilities such as a café and public toilets, while one gallery was converted into a cased display area for applied art objects. In the remaining art galleries a new daylighting system, based on recommendations for the reconstruction of the National Gallery made by F. P. Cockerell as long ago as 1850, was introduced.

The final stages of conversion of the Industrial Hall, 1950.

The reconstructed galleries were opened in 1958, bringing to an end a long period of upheaval in the Central Museum. There had been other changes occurring in the building. The loss of galleries for wartime uses did at least provide the opportunity to introduce changes as the galleries were released for museum use again. The picture galleries were in much the same form as before the war but the applied art, natural history and archaeological galleries had to be re-displayed before they could be opened to the public again. The most startling example of this process was the Industrial Hall, re-opened in January 1951. It had been 'transformed' by the insertion of a suspended ceiling and modern displays for the ceramic and textile collections.

The staff of the Natural History Department were also pre-occupied after the war with preparing their galleries for re-opening. The first two were ready for visitors in 1946-7 and included the very popular domed

Carved argillite bowl, an example of North American Indian art.

Etrusco-Corinthian scent bottle in the form of a hind, c.600-550 BC.

gallery. The refurbishment of the exhibits from the old collections for new displays must have absorbed much staff time. In April 1948 the Beale Gallery of birds was opened after blast-damaged exhibits had been restored. These displays were unaltered in their presentation from pre-War days. In January 1949 the Chase Collection of Birds, re-displayed as a large gallery, was once again on show, and in June 1951 the Ethnographical Gallery was re-opened. In 1954 Cannon Hill re-opened as a branch museum of Natural History. Its instructive displays were popular and within five years attendances were exceeding 100,000 visitors annually. Finally, in March 1955, a new Geology Gallery was opened which employed a thematic and didactic treatment of the subject, heralding a new era in 'educational displays'.

To these Central Museum developments must be added the creation of the Birmingham Museum of Science and Industry. The City's industrial heritage made such a museum essential and a few items had been collected before the war but much more had been promised on condition of the idea becoming reality. In July 1949 the City Council committed itself to finding a building suitable for the museum. It was eventually decided to purchase a factory in Newhall Street being vacated by Elkingtons, the silver plate manufacturers. The first gallery, containing the 'Museum of Arms' (which had been in store since 1939), was opened in the summer of 1951. Further galleries were opened thereafter to cover a wide range of scientific and industrial subject matter. In 1983 a major extension, the James Watt Building, was opened, including the 'Smethwick Engine', a 1779 Boulton and Watt steam engine used for pumping water up canal locks at Smethwick.

As one approaches the present day it obviously becomes more and more difficult to identify those developments which may be considered important in the growth of Birmingham Museum and Art Gallery. Since Trenchard Cox departed to become Director of the Victoria and Albert Museum in 1956 there have been four Directors at Birmingham: Mary Woodall (1956-63); John Lowe (1963-69); Dennis Farr (1969-80) and Michael Diamond (the present incumbent). This relatively frequent turnover in some ways reflects how the museums profession as a whole was expanding, allowing far greater career opportunity and staff mobility. With this expansion came not only changes in methods but also the growing importance of non-curatorial staff in the provision of a good museums service.

Museums in general in the 1960s and 1970s were paying greater attention to 'interpretation' and to 'relating to local communities', rather than to the building up of academically excellent collections. This movement manifested itself in a number of different ways at Birmingham. In 1964 a Schools Liaison Service was set up which helped teachers to use the Museum and also provided classroom facilities. Over a period of twenty years this service grew and came to be a key element in the promotion of both informal and formal education for adults and children alike. The presentation of the galleries had largely been a curatorial matter before the 1970s but then, in common with many other museums, Birmingham established a Design and Display Unit. Headed by a professional designer, this was entrusted with the task of improving the quality of displays in the galleries.

There were also changes in curatorial objectives during this period: the Natural History Department, for example, took a much greater interest in fieldwork and recording by observation than in the mere collecting of specimens. This trend in museums generally was partly in response to the spread and growing influence of organisations for the conservation of wildlife. The Department began to use sound recording equipment outdoors in 1958 and started to engage in surveys of local fauna and flora. It also began aiding or co-operating with societies whose aims now more often precluded the collection of specimens. The formation of the Nature Centre (opened in 1975) was a bold step further in this direction, attempting to bring facets of the countryside and its wildlife actually into the city as a live demonstration of animal behaviour in quasi-natural habitats. Its success in attracting visitors exceeded that of the neighbouring Cannon Hill Museum (finally closed in 1977) which it replaced as a museum development more in tune with the changing public attitude to natural history.

Similarly, Birmingham was not unaffected by the

Guiding a school party at the Nature Centre.

Dealing with the bees at the Nature Centre.

spectacular rise in public interest in local history. Adrian Oswald, the Keeper of Archaeology, is quoted as saying in 1950 that 'Birmingham Art Gallery may be called the British Museum of the Midlands'. Others have pointed out that the archaeological collections at least did not merit such a claim. It is nevertheless broadly true that much of what was attempted in Birmingham was in imitation of what was done at the National Museums in Bloomsbury and South Kensington. This is, of course, hardly surprising. Many provincial museums and art galleries were headed by men who had received their early training in London. Furthermore the Museum had been founded on the basis that its collections should be drawn from wherever objects of quality could be found which would assist in the improvement of industrial design in Birmingham. Under these circumstances it was inevitable that Birmingham Museum should be much more than just a 'local museum'. Unfortunately, before the 1970s, the 'local' element hardly surfaced among all the universal culture.

The development of 'universal collections' has been justified on the grounds that not everyone can or wishes to travel to London to see examples of culture and natural science from all over the world. Nicholas Thomas, whilst dismissing any suggestion that Birmingham is a 'minor British Museum', has pointed out that for 'the museum-going public of the Midlands, anxious for at least a glimpse of the achievements of the great civilizations of the world, there is . . . justification for building a collection of antiquities in Birmingham whose scope is altogether wider than that to which most . . . museums limit themselves'. This reasoning is sound and has been essentially the justification for the Museum's collecting policies throughout its existence. Nevertheless, it made little allowance for the fact that many visitors were actually interested not in the wider world but in their own particular corner of it.

In 1895 it was observed that 'The time may come when a room in the extended Municipal Museum and Art Gallery may be devoted to the illustration of Birmingham history. When the long-looked-for day arrives, it will be found . . . that there exists a very considerable nucleus of such a collection'. That 'long-looked-for day' did not arrive until 4 June 1981 when

Birmingham Police pistol, 1840.

Burnished pottery ritual chalice from Vounous, Cyprus.

Selective purchases continue to develop the numismatic collections. Gold ryal of Coventry, 1465.

(opposite) Egyptian funeral bust of a nobleman.

The Local History Gallery, opened in 1981.

Pewter communion cruet from
Weoley Castle.

the Local History Gallery was opened. Birmingham
material had not been entirely neglected before this
period, but neither had it been recognised as having a
value simply through its association with the city.
Such collections were kept by the Department of
Archaeology, and a member of staff with sole responsibility for Birmingham history was not appointed until
1969. The Department of Art and the Museum of
Science and Industry also held material relating to
Birmingham but neither displayed their collections
with the Birmingham connection as the main feature.

Some local archaeological material had always been
displayed in the Central Museum along with local
metalwork. Blakesley Hall was opened in 1935 as a
museum of manorial history but the local history
potential of the building was not exploited. A small
'museum' was built at Weoley Castle in 1960 but has
always been somewhat of a backwater. In 1969

The 'Warwick Vase' on a trade card of
George Collis.

(*left*) Fieldwork takes the Museum's local
historians to some curious places.

Sarehole Mill, the last surviving water corn mill in the
Birmingham area, was opened as a branch museum.
Its building dates from the eighteenth century and its
history reflects the industrial history of the city, its rural
past and the impact of suburbanisation. Sarehole
represented both the increasing interest in local history
and the trend towards the creation of 'site' museums.

Nevertheless, the history of Birmingham itself still
remained untold in Birmingham Museum. Throughout
the 1970s a programme of fieldwork added well-
documented local history material to the collections,
while a programme of exhibitions and lectures brought
to life the history of Birmingham for the city's own
people. In 1980 a separate Department of Local
History (the Keeper of which, Stephen Price, had
joined the Museum in 1973) was formed and the Local
History Gallery was opened in the following year.
In the early 1980s Blakesley Hall has been re-displayed

One of a pair of patent chimney
ornaments made by Benjamin Day of
Snow Hill, Birmingham, c.1820.

Recording where past and present meet, this photograph by Celia Grant was part of a project to record 'Change in the Inner City'.

as a period house based on its own documentation with supporting displays on themes of suburban history. A Sound Archive has been established to record the memories of Birmingham people in respect of several subjects, many of which relate to Birmingham's inner city areas.

The effect of the increase in the appeal of local history and the movement towards interpreting historic houses through their own history can also be seen in the development of Aston Hall as a branch museum. Aston Hall is a large early-seventeenth-century country house standing in the surviving portion of its park (originally over five times its present extent), about 2½ miles north of central Birmingham. Begun in 1618 and largely complete by 1635, it is a surprisingly grandiose brick house with stone dressings, firmly Jacobean in style with a dramatic skyline of shaped gables, tall chimneys and turrets. Built by Sir Thomas Holte, a successful north Warwickshire squire, it is a building of considerable architectural quality, described by a contemporary as 'a noble fabric which for beauty and state much exceedeth any in these parts'. Inside a good deal of fine early-seventeenth-century ornament survives. The highly ornate long gallery and great staircase have remained almost unchanged, and the house has a distinguished series of moulded plaster ceilings and of sandstone and alabaster chimney pieces.

The Holte family kept Aston Hall until 1817 when they sold it to a firm of bankers who let it out to James Watt's son. After his death, in 1849, the house was emptied of its contents and another suitable tenant could not be found. Over the next ten years the south and west part of Aston Park (hitherto preserved intact) began to be sold off for housing and the future of the Hall itself was in doubt. Following the passing of the *Birmingham Parks Act* of 1854 the Corporation did try to acquire it but negotiations came to nothing. Two fêtes held in the park in 1856 to raise funds for the Birmingham General Hospital raised a good deal of interest in the future of the house and park, neither of which had ever been open to the Birmingham public. In June 1857 a public meeting called to save Aston Hall led to the formation of an artisans committee, which subsequently decided to try to buy the house outright. Having become a private company as the Aston Hall and Park Company Ltd., they agreed in March 1858 to purchase the house and 43 acres of the park for the sum of £35,000. They decided to use the house as a museum and exhibition gallery, assembling an exhibition of manufactures and art treasures in the spirit of the Great Exhibition of 1851; and a glass pavilion in the 'Elizabethan style' was built against the west front. Aston Hall and Park was opened to the public by Queen Victoria on 15 June 1858.

From 1860 more and more of the house was used for semi-permanent tableaux, with scenes of eskimo life (from which a genuine eskimo kayak survives in the

Eskimo kayak, formerly at Aston Hall.

The Great Hall, Aston Hall, 1984.

collections of the Department of Archaeology and Ethnography) in the chapel and adjoining colonnade room, a stalactite cave in the green library, and a Chinese street scene in the small dining room, complete with a barber shaving a customer's head. By 1863 there were also displays of botanical specimens, ethnographic weapons, stuffed birds and Indian handcrafts, and the Company had (perhaps inadvertently) acquired the nucleus of a museum collection, variously by gift, long loan and purchase.

Nevertheless, it had its critics who regarded its fund-raising activities as 'pandering to the demands for the sensational and vulgar'. In the latter part of 1864 it was unable to survive a financial crisis and a public scandal resulting from the death of a female acrobat during a fête in the park. The Council finally took over the Company and re-opened Aston Hall and Park to the public on 22 September 1864. Aston Hall thus became the first historic country house to pass into municipal ownership. Birmingham's lead was to be followed by many other local authorities during the next seventy years or so as large historic houses were overtaken by urban expansion and utilised as museums.

From 1864 Aston Hall was administered by the Corporation's Superintendent of Parks, who occupied part of the south wing. In 1872 a number of Holte family portraits and other heirlooms, some already on loan to the house, passed to the Corporation under the will of Charles Holte Bracebridge, the grandson of the last baronet. In 1885 Aston Hall became one of the responsibilities of Whitworth Wallis. During his long directorship the glass pavilion was demolished, and the surviving displays prepared during the Aston Hall and Park Co. period were removed. Wallis apparently (and quite reasonably) regarded the Company's activities as frivolous and inappropriate, and many of his alterations (the removal of stuffed animals from the great hall for example) were sensible, but one feels that during the first quarter of this century Aston Hall was a somewhat characterless annexe to the City Museum and Art Gallery, with displays of oriental objects, ethnographic weapons, local history objects, nineteenth-century paintings and engravings, and the collection of the British and foreign birds. Aston Park was also somewhat neglected during this period, and became the subject of improvements initiated and partly funded by the Birmingham Civic Society between 1918 and 1934. As early as 1925 Whitworth Wallis agreed to the Civic Society's proposal that changes should be made in the interior arrangement of the Hall in order to bring it as near as possible to the condition of a furnished mansion of the period (the early seventeenth century). Little was achieved, however, before 1939, when Aston Hall was evacuated. Though near-missed by bombs the house survived the war almost unscathed.

In 1949 a serious outbreak of dry rot was discovered on the west side of the house. A structural survey revealed many other problems, and restoration work continued in several phases for over ten years. Both Trenchard Cox and Mary Woodall felt that Aston Hall was a building of quite exceptional architectural quality, and that its only appropriate use was as a show place for fine furniture and paintings of the seventeenth, eighteenth and early-nineteenth centuries. During this period a number of important country house collections had been put in store by their owners, and material from several of these was borrowed for display at Aston Hall. Meanwhile the Museum was for the first time trying to acquire a representative collection of English furniture, and from 1949 two or three objects were bought in most years, generally from the principal London dealers of the day. Purchases were to include a late-sixteenth-century chestnut table-frame with an Italian top of inlaid marble, a walnut and oak frame table of the same period, some important examples of seventeenth-century upholstered seat furniture, and a number of early-eighteenth-century walnut and japanned pieces − most of these objects which now (1984) have passed out of the museum's price range. This policy was also to attract several significant gifts and bequests, among them a walnut marquetry cabinet of *c.*1690 from J. R. H. Sumner, a large mahogany bureau bookcase of *c.*1800 from Mrs W. A. Cadbury, and over a dozen good seventeenth- and eighteenth-century pieces from Captain G. Morris RN. By 1960 Aston Hall had been largely refurnished after standing half empty for over a hundred years and the last 'museum' displays were removed.

The Green Library, Aston Hall, 1984.

Embroidered carpet of the 1760s, including the Holte coat of arms.

The Kitchen, Aston Hall.

Thereafter the resources allocated to Aston Hall were again (and understandably) allowed to dwindle. Unfortunately several major loan collections were also withdrawn from the house in the 1960s and 1970s either for sale or to return to their former homes, some of which had now been opened to the public by their owners. Meanwhile the Aston district of Birmingham, traditionally one of small industrial concerns and low-cost housing, entered a period of urban decay. Many of the late Victorian terraces around Aston Park were demolished and an urban motorway, the A38(M), was built only a few hundred yards from Aston Hall. By the early 1970s it was felt that the policy of using Aston Hall as a showplace for fine furniture and paintings was no longer reasonable, and designers were commissioned to turn the house into a museum of British Art, involving the construction of cased displays for much of the Gallery's applied art collections. However, funds for this project were not forthcoming.

By 1974 the condition of the Hall was once again giving cause for alarm. At the same time curatorial opinion as to how such houses should be presented to the public was changing. It was therefore decided to appoint an additional Assistant Keeper specifically to research the history of the Hall and its owners and to reorganise the displays in such a way as to make them more closely faithful to that history. It has proved possible to establish the original plan of the house, as well as a good deal about its mid-seventeenth-century furnishing and use, and to chart how the building was gradually adapted to reflect changes in fashion and in social patterns up to the 1760s. Thereafter the house underwent almost no significant changes, making it an architectural and social document of the greatest importance.

Because it was felt that the museum's furniture collections should remain at Aston Hall, work began on their rearrangement to reflect what was now known of how the building was furnished at various dates in the past. It thus remained as a series of furnished rooms, but of rooms which tell visitors something of how Aston Hall functioned as a house and to reflect recent research by furniture historians on how interiors were arranged and used in the seventeenth and eighteenth centuries.

Between late 1982 and 1984 the Hall was closed for major structural and service repairs. As floorboards and panelling had to be removed throughout the house for re-wiring, there was an invaluable opportunity to study concealed structural details and fragments of early decoration, adding further to our understanding of the building's development. Fourteen rooms were redecorated; where possible use was made of the evidence provided by the study of the paint layers which had survived early-twentieth-century paint stripping, supplemented by early-nineteenth-century views and surveys. When this was completed the contents of the house, supplemented by further paintings from the Museum's collections and by a number of purchases, were rearranged along the lines described above. Aston Hall was then reopened to the public on 17 April 1984.

Another major project of the early 1980s was the refurbishment of the original galleries of 1885. The centrepiece of these was the Industrial Hall. It was open to a roof of glass supported by iron trusses raised upon columns. Two side balconies were originally reached by four corner spiral staircases. Before the Great War two additional end galleries and a new central staircase were added. These features were all largely hidden after 1950 when a suspended ceiling was installed and the space used for 'modern' displays, stores, workshops and offices. By the end of the 1970s this area was in need of refurbishment.

The decision to reveal and restore the original nineteenth-century architecture was influenced by the revival of interest in the Victorian period, promoted in Birmingham by the local branch of the Victorian Society and a number of the museum's own staff whose interests lay in that period. There was also very much a feeling of returning to the original spirit of the building. The new displays were to be primarily of the applied art collections, including the 'industrial art' so avidly collected in the early days. Even the new cases were to be arranged in a manner reminiscent of the 1880s. Finally the whole project perhaps also recognised the fact that a museum's buildings are among the foremost 'objects' in the collections and ought to be given due attention.

There have been major advances in how collections

Exhibition in converted Industrial Hall, c.1954.

Rhyl Sands, one of the J. H. Nettlefold
bequest of David Cox paintings.

(opposite) Ancient Egyptian coffin;
painted plaster on wood. XXVI dynasty or
later, 600-300BC.

have been interpreted and displayed since the 1960s,
but perhaps the single most important achievement of
that period relates to the care of collections, which is,
of course, fundamental to the existence of any museum.
The necessity for preservation of the exhibits became
apparent almost as soon as a public art collection had
been formed in Birmingham. In May 1868 the cele-
brated Sultanganj Buddha, presented to the town by
Samuel Thornton the year before and set up in the Art
Gallery at the Midland Institute, was reported to have
'cracked in various directions', owing to its great weight
and it had subsequently to be laid down on the gallery
floor pending repairs.

Following the opening of the Corporation Free Art
Gallery in 1867, concern was expressed of the effect on
the exhibits of air pollution, sunlight, and fumes from
the coal-gas lighting. Despite the introduction into the
new Museum and Art Gallery of a measure of electric
lighting as early as 1894, gas persisted for many years
as the primary source of illumination. Reservations
continued to be expressed about the deleterious effects
of gas fumes and, in an attempt to dispel these fears, in
1903 the Museum and Art Gallery Committee commissioned an investigation into the atmosphere of
the Long Gallery under gas and electrical illumination
respectively. The terms of the Nettlefold bequest of Cox

paintings (1882) required that they should only be exhibited illuminated by electricity and, following refusal by the Nettlefold Trustees to waive this stipulation, the Round Gallery was fitted out to house these paintings with electric lighting powered from the Corporation's own supply main.

Little is recorded during these times about the physical preservation or care of the collections, although doubtless such work was carried out by the Keeper and his staff, or by outside specialists. Between 1899 and 1919, for instance, the natural history collections at Aston Hall were periodically examined and treated by a consulting taxidermist.

Development of the Museum and Art Gallery, the expansion of its collections, staff and activities placed increasing pressure on both available space and finance until, by the middle of the twentieth century, a state of crisis had arisen throughout all departments, but especially in the storage and care of the art collections.

Conservation of museum exhibits, the collective process of cleaning, preservation and restoration really became a major issue in museum philosophy only after the Second World War, largely as the result of national and international attention and scientific research into the subject. Birmingham was slow to respond to the challenge presented by this philosophical change in attitude until reports by the Keeper of Art and of the then newly appointed Director (Dennis Farr) were presented to Committee in 1969 uncompromisingly setting out the position.

All Departments, with the exception of Art, had some conservation facilities and staff on the premises, although nothing like sufficient to meet the needs of collections amassed over three-quarters of a century. Such work as was carried out on oil paintings was in the hands of an internationally renowned consulting restorer, Mr Herbert Lank, but only a limited amount of his time could be placed at Birmingham's disposal. Works restored by him were being returned to totally unsatisfactory environmental conditions in the galleries to begin deteriorating once more.

Storage of the art collections was hopelessly inadequate; the oil paintings store, for instance, was being used as a main thoroughfare by caterers supplying the

A wassail bowl from the Pinto Collection.

Museum café and on occasions as a food preparation area for civic banquets. With the exception of the Pinto Gallery, none of the storage areas or galleries were air-conditioned or even thermostatically controlled. Rapid fluctuations of temperature and relative humidity were imposing unacceptable strains on fragile materials, especially panel paintings and veneered furniture. The effects of air pollution on the collections were also pointed out.

During the following year these problems received extensive press coverage culminating in a sensational article on the 'National Scandal of Birmingham's Rotting Art Treasures'; 'Birmingham . . . which has many important works of art on loan, is shamed by the fact that an art expert has described the situation as so bad that he cannot advise a private owner to lend his pictures to the gallery. If this is so, it is more than a local issue. It is a national scandal'. Lord Clarke, former Chairman of the Arts Council, lecturing at the Museum, commented that 'the gallery is not worthy of its excellent collections' while the Chairman of National Heritage – reporting that almost half the museum collections in Britain were deteriorating, in some cases rapidly – singled out Birmingham for specially adverse comment. Fuel was added to the fire of indignation when a seventeenth-century tapestry after a design by Raphael, collapsed at Aston Hall, allegedly because atmospheric pollution had caused the fibres to give way.

Specialist advice was rapidly mustered; Mr Garry Thomson, Scientific Adviser to the National Gallery, reported on the environmental implications; Mr Eric Harding, Senior Conservation Officer at the British Museum, reported on the problems of the prints, drawings and watercolours collection; and a commercial specialist provided details of environmental control equipment required. A number of the galleries were closed to allow work to be carried out on art affected by bad storage conditions and sixteen mobile electric humidifiers were installed in the picture galleries and art stores as a temporary measure to combat low humidity conditions. Questions asked in the House of Commons regarding the training of art restorers and the annual loss to be attributed to the decay of works of art in public ownership and in need of conservation cited the problems of Birmingham Museum and Art Gallery in both respects.

Subsequently steps were taken to provide a purpose-built air-conditioned store for the prints, drawings and watercolours collections, and more adequate storage for the oil paintings collection, both at the expense of display space. Commenting to the press, the Director said that 'a gallery containing a collection of perishable artefacts must keep them in a good state of repair. Preservation may not be spectacular or exciting but it is an absolutely essential activity'.

At the time, no one person had overall responsibility for conservation of the collections. Following a submission in 1970, the decision was made to set up a centralised Conservation department on the lines already well established in National collections and currently becoming more usual in major provincial museums. In October 1971, the first Keeper of Conservation, Mr Stephen G. Rees-Jones, was appointed with the mandate to set up a department suitable to serve the needs of the collections at Birmingham.

Plans to eliminate the harmful natural daylight from two galleries to provide safe display space for watercolours by replacement of the roof-lights with slate were later modified by a programme of work substantially to reduce glazing in the gallery laylights, a programme which is now being implemented in other picture galleries today. Less satisfactorily, the proposals for full air-conditioning of the galleries and storage areas were never accepted because of cost, so that the initial temporary solution involving the use of mobile humidifiers (with all the limitations and constraints which this solution involves) has now become permanent. Monitoring and control of environmental conditions to alleviate excessive dryness is now an essential part of the Department's activities, although little can be done about the corrosive and soiling effects of air pollution. By 1974, vandalism in the galleries intensified the programme of glazing oil paintings on display, already implemented to protect them from becoming soiled.

Because of the nature of its work the Conservation Department is fully involved in the activities of the Museum and Art Gallery. A continuing policy of

This Old Master print by Beham came to Birmingham in 1968 from the Thomas Balston bequest and through the National Art Collections Fund.

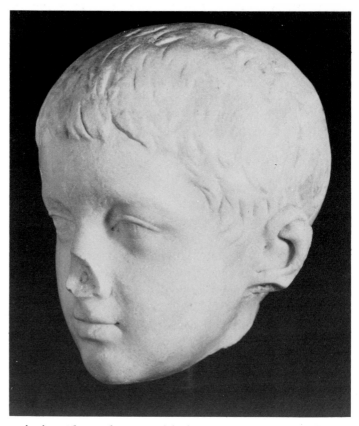

Many of the Museum's objects cross discipline boundaries. This piece of sculpture, marble bust of a boy, is Roman.

paintings' loans has provided a constant stream of requests for examination and conservation, and vast amounts of material have been prepared for major exhibitions and re-displays such as the Local History Gallery (1981), the Industrial Gallery (1984), and the re-display of Aston Hall (1984).

The nature of conservation work means that few members of the public are aware that it is a continuing process throughout all the collections. The Ottoni bust of Cardinal Mattei, completely smashed by a vandal in 1974, was restored in the Conservation Department in such a way that it can now be displayed again as if complete. The restoration of many other important paintings and objects passes unnoticed by the majority of visitors.

In reviewing the history of Birmingham Museum and Art Gallery since the Second World War one ought to draw attention to three important features. The first is the growth in numbers of professional staff, including not only the curators but also those of the 'support services' built up in the 1970s. Additional curators have

Special exhibitions are an important element in Birmingham Museum's service to the public.

made greater specialisation possible which has in turn allowed the collections to be academically assessed and arranged. Other professionals have then assisted in the conservation, display and publication of these collections for the greater benefit of the visiting public.

Secondly, the middle part of the century had perhaps seen a drift away from the strong identification which the Museum and Art Gallery had with Birmingham itself in the nineteenth century. In the 1950s and 1960s the Art Gallery in particular had aspired to an 'international' outlook. This trend was halted and in large measure reversed in the 1970s and 1980s. The change cannot be explained simply by the growth of interest in local history and the attention which the Gallery's art historians now gave to the 'Birmingham School' of artists of all kinds, though both were important. Beyond this one may discern a greater recognition of the need for the Museum to 'belong' to Birmingham.

Finally, in the last few years in particular, there has been a growing awareness among local politicians that the Museum and Art Gallery has an important role to play in the development of a corporate image and in the civic life of the city. This encompasses its place as an attraction for tourists but goes beyond it as well. The Museum and Art Gallery's quality and appeal is important in sustaining Birmingham's position as Britain's 'Second City' and the leading regional capital. This link between the Museum and civic pride has been an enduring one despite a history of changing emphases and fashions. Today, however, its place in the public life of Birmingham is greater than ever before, a true indication of just how much its curators, benefactors and supporters have achieved since the idea was first mooted one hundred and forty years ago.

Select Bibliography

The principal 'primary' sources consulted have been the printed Council Minutes ('Birmingham Council Proceedings'), the manuscript Committee Minute Books (held by the City's Archives Department), newspaper files, the museum's own archives (including letters and other documentation relating to the collections), exhibition catalogues and guide books. For the post-war period the recollections of some former members of staff have also been drawn upon.

R. C. Barnett, P. Klein & N. Thomas, 'A new gallery at Birmingham City Museum for the Pinto Collection of Treen', *The Museums Journal*, 70 (1), (June 1970), 24-28.

N. W. Bertenshaw, 'The Birmingham Museum of Science and Industry', *Junior Institution of Engineers*, (1962), 128-138.

A. Briggs, *History of Birmingham*, ii, (1952).

J. T. Bunce, *History of the Corporation of Birmingham*, i & ii, (1878 and 1885).

A. B. Chamberlain, 'The Corporation Museum and Art Gallery', in G. A. Auden (ed.), *A Handbook for Birmingham*, (British Association for the Advancement of Science, 1913).

S. Dalby, 'A Problem of Display', *The Museums Journal*, 83 (2/3), (Sept./Dec. 1983), 151-155.

S. Davies, *Birmingham Museum and Art Gallery*, Department of Local History Information Sheet no. 9, (1981).

S. Davies, 'Birmingham's Local History Gallery', *The Museums Journal*, 81 (3), (Dec. 1981), 159-163.

S. Davies & D. Symons, 'Birmingham's Coin Gallery', *The Museums Journal*, 82 (4), (Mar. 1983), 233-235.

S. Davies, *Sarehole Mill*, Department of Local History Information Sheet, no. 14 (1984).

O. Fairclough, *The Grand Old Mansion: The Holtes and Their Successors at Aston Hall 1618-1864* (1983).

D. Farr, 'Local History in Birmingham', *The Museums Journal*, 82 (4), (Mar. 1983), 247.

A. Gunstone, 'Local History in Birmingham: Review and Reminiscence', *The Museums Journal*, 82 (3), (Dec. 1982), 180-182.

P. Hanney, 'A new Bird Gallery at Birmingham',
   The Museums Journal, 68 (4), (Mar. 1969), 165-167.

K. Hull, 'Birmingham City Museum and Art Gallery',
   Unpublished Dissertation, (Oxford Polytechnic, 1983).

J. T. Jones, *History of the Corporation of Birmingham*,
   v, (part 2), (1940).

G. Kavanagh, 'Museums, Memorials and Minenwerfers',
   The Museums Journal, 84, (2), (Sept. 1984), 65-70.

K. L. Kenrick, *Birmingham Natural History and
   Philosophical Society. The Records of the Society
   and the Story They Tell* (1958).

J. A. Langford, *Modern Birmingham and its Institutions,
   1841 to 1871* (1911).

G. Learmonth, *Thomason's 'Warwick Vase'*, Department of
   Local History Information Sheet no. 11 (1981).

R. Ormond, 'Victorian Paintings and Patronage in
   Birmingham', *Apollo*, (April 1968), 240-251.

D. Payler, 'Display and Labelling', *The Museums Journal*,
   33 (1), (May 1933), 41-44.

A. G. Sheppard Fidler, 'Reconstruction at Birmingham City
   Museum and Art Gallery', *Birmingham Five Counties
   Architectural Association Green Book*, (1959-60), 67-71.

V. Skipp, *The Making of Victorian Birmingham*, (1983).

N. Thomas, 'Archaeology at the Birmingham City Museum
   – Retrospect and Prospect', *Alta*, (Spring 1969), 82-86.

N. Thomas & J. Ruffle, 'Ancient Life in Miniature: the
   anatomy of an exhibition', *The Museums Journal*, 69 (2),
   (Sept. 1969), 58-62.

C. A. Vince, *History of the Corporation of Birmingham*,
   iii & iv, (1902 & 1923).

E. W. Vincent, *Notable Pictures*, (1949).

W. Wallis, 'The Museum and Art Gallery', in J. H. Muirhead,
   Birmingham Institutions, (1911), 475-521.

R. E. Waterhouse, *The Birmingham and Midland Institute*
   (1954).

H. R. G. Whates, *The Birmingham Post 1857-1957*, (1957).

G. Wild, 'English and Continental Silver in the Godman
   Collection', *Apollo*, (April 1968), 266-273.

H. Willoughby Ellis, 'Presidential Address', *Proceedings of
   the Birmingham Natural History and Philosophical
   Society*, xii, (4), (1910).

Details from watercolour drawings of the Art Gallery, prepared at the time of its opening.

(right) Weoley Castle.
(below) Aston Hall.

(opposite, above) Blakesley Hall.
(opposite, below) Sarehole Mill.

(right) The Nature Centre, Cannon Hill.
(below) The Birmingham Museum of
Science and Industry.

(opposite, above) William Holman Hunt
(1827-1910), *Two Gentlemen of Verona.*
(opposite, below) Orazio Gentileschi
(1562-1647), *The Rest on the Flight into
Egypt.*

Arthur Hughes (1832-1915), *The Long Engagement:* one of the many Pre-Raphaelite paintings acquired before the Great War.

(opposite) Carlo Dolci (1616-1686), *St Andrew Praying Before his Martyrdom.*

The Sultanganj Buddha, the Museum's
first acquisition.

(opposite) Hilaire-Germain-Edgar Degas
(1834-1917), *Roman Beggar Woman*,
painted in 1857.

(right) Items from the Applied Art
Collections.

(below) David Cox (1783-1859),
The Horsefair. A Birmingham artist and
subject.

A miniature portrait of James Bisset.

A rare specimen of the extinct Philip Island Parrot.

Contemporary crafts continue to be
represented in the Museum's Collections.
(below) Japanned tray showing the Bull
Ring and St Martin's.

(opposite) Hans Memling (1430/5-1494),
Nativity.

'The Dinosaur' is, ironically, perhaps the single most popular 'object' in the Museum.

John Baskerville's portrait on a
papier-mâché snuff box.

A mask from the Ethnographical
Collections.

(right) The newly-refurbished Industrial Gallery.
(below) Items from the Applied Art Collections.

(opposite) Alfred Sisley (1839-1899), *La Vieille Eglise de Moret*. Presented by the Public Picture Gallery Fund in 1948.

The Ship by Edward Burne-Jones (1833-1898).

(opposite) Corals and birds from the Natural History Collections.

Ford Madox Brown (1821-1893), *The Last of England*. Purchased in 1891, this may claim to be Birmingham's most famous picture.